# Physics of Correspondence: Wholeness

Janey Marvin

*Physics of Correspondence: Wholeness*

Copyright © 2021 by Janey Marvin.

Paperback ISBN: 978-1-63812-054-4
Hardcover ISBN: 978-1-63812-056-8
Ebook ISBN: 978-1-63812-055-1

All rights reserved. No part in this book may be produced and transmitted in any form or by any means, electronic, or mechanical, including photocopying, recording, or by any information storage and retrieval system, without permission in writing from the copyright owner.

The views expressed in this work are solely those of the author and do not necessarily reflect the views of the publisher hereby disclaims any responsibility for them.

Published by Pen Culture Solutions   06/28/2021

Pen Culture Solutions
1-888-727-7204 (USA)
1-800-950-458 (Australia)
support@penculturesolutions.com

# Contents

| | | |
|---|---|---|
| Chapter 1 | Physics Laws of Correspondence | 1 |
| Chapter 2 | Function "of" Origin and Purpose | 6 |
| Chapter 3 | Mathematics of Function | 11 |
| Chapter 4 | Elements of Correspondence | 17 |
| Chapter 5 | Function: Purpose of Action for which Something Exists | 22 |
| Chapter 6 | Gravitation and Related Acceleration Phenomena | 29 |
| Chapter 7 | Human Transformation Theory | 36 |
| Chapter 8 | Reality Principle and Transformation | 44 |
| Chapter 9 | Fields of Human Consciousness | 50 |
| Chapter 10 | Totalities of Transformation Theory | 54 |
| Chapter 11 | Sensory Firing Orders | 64 |
| Chapter 12 | Quantum Leaps | 75 |
| Chapter 13 | Memory-Correspondence | 91 |
| Chapter 14 | Inner Unification | 98 |
| Chapter 15 | Exchange of Energy is Discontinuous | 118 |
| Chapter 16 | "S" Curve | 131 |
| Chapter 17 | Totality Transformation Theory | 151 |
| Chapter 18 | Being Leads to Having | 180 |
| Chapter 19 | Bridging the Quantums | 192 |
| Chapter 20 | Algorithm of Elements | 201 |
| Chapter 21 | Choice | 211 |

# Introduction

Physics of Correspondence "Wholeness" originates from the Holographic Human Transformation Theory. Holographic Human Transformation Theory incorporates wisdoms of the ancient Greeks and is based upon three simple words at the entrance of the Temple of Delphi: Know Thy Self.

Holographic Human Theory gives us knowledge of our inner world, our subconscious self which has been directing our lives throughout all mortality. All of our fears, hatred, envying, sorrows, anxieties, everything we thought to be a part of us and the world. Everything we experience as our Reality, Identity, IQ, Emotion, Thought, Physical, and all of our being is subconscious programming. The Greek knew this, and they knew the inner-beings Nature; It's Structure, its Patterns, and its Processes. Holographic Human Theory and Transformation Theory is knowledge shared by the ancient Greeks from the Temple of Delphi.

I have studied Holographic Human Theory since 1996 after attending a weekend training from Michael Miller on it. Something about it, I could not put it down. I researched every single word in his book I received from the training that had to do with Holographic Human Theory. Including simple words such as "it", "of", "is", "as". I researched words I had never used before. I researched in dictionaries, thesauruses, scriptures, physics, and quantum physics. I researched Einstein, Max Planck, Thomas Kuhn, and many other physicists whose works the research lead me to. My research process consisted of first gathering Data from any and all sources corresponding with my scriptural researching and knowledge. After gathering the Data of each and every word, I took the data of each word and then wrote a dialogue of information from the data of the word, and created theories corresponding with the Holographic Human. Lastly, I practiced and applied the information and theories from the data and dialogue and repeated from step one of my research, gathering any new Data I ran into during the implementing stage, this leads to greater knowledge.

This book is one of many books I have written and will continue to write regarding Holographic Human and Holographic Human Transformation Theory because the information is copious.

Holographic Human Theory consists of many different natures of Know Thy Self: Linguistics, CNS neuron-firings, 7- human senses, their functions, intelligence, each body organ and system, it's abstract function and individual intelligence, and the nature all of this corresponds together to make us Be. Much that is not run by conscious was known by the ancient Greeks and is passed on in the Holographic Human Theory. Holographic Human Theory teaches you to recognize all of these subconscious functions, to know their intelligences and nature. To "Know Thy Self". It teaches you, along with the techniques I have developed based upon their functions the way to "Heal Thy Self".

All conscious functions are for our being to perceive what subconscious tells it to, to evaluate it, to judge it, and then to decide about it. Everything else we have known as Self, is just subconscious program. Even what conscious gets to perceive about.

I have done this now since 1996. I have thousands of papers and illustrations; I have taught it as part of our educational class in our treatment facility (MATR Behavioral Health in Mt. Pleasant Utah). I am writing books for other professionals and anyone interested. I have created hundreds of experiential techniques to apply the information more easily in group and individual settings. I do trainings, coaching. I have worked in Human Services since 1976. I have owned and operated my own treatment program since 1993. I received my Master in Hypnotherapy and Certified with the International Medical Dental Hypnotherapy Association in

Hypno-anesthesia in 1996. I was one of three people west of the Mississippi certified by them to do Hypno-anesthesia. I had to learn the structure, patterns, and processes of brain and body organ and system functions and correspondence and conscious consequences. Already knowing these things then just a weekend training of Holographic Human and I knew there was more of greater value than had been recognized yet.

I love the work I do. I love believing when a person knows the path to help them to become a greater being, they will choose it.

"I believe in God, the Eternal Father and in His Son, Jesus Christ and in the Holy Ghost.", the First Article of Faith of the Church of Jesus Christ of Latter-Day Saints. I believe we are all God's children. I believe it is His work and His glory to "bring to pass the immortality and eternal life of man".

He gave us all the Gospel of Jesus Christ of Latter-Day Saints, He created us to return to Him for immortality and eternal life. I believe "a man cannot be saved in ignorance", D&C 131:6. I believe "If there is anything virtuous, lovely or of good report, we seek after these things", Thirteenth Article of Faith of the Church of Jesus Christ of Latter-Day Saints.

I believe that Lucifer will give you 99 truths to get you to believe 1 lie. The scriptures are a significant resource of my research.

Holographic Human Theory and Holographic Human Transformation Theory teaches about your inner self, the self that has been a mystery to us all for most of our mortality. The consequences of not knowing thy self (our subconscious programs) is despair, hurt, disease, depression, and all the mortal problems whether mental, emotional, or physical are the consequences of not knowing our inner self.

Wholeness is one aspect of Holographic Human Transformation Theory. Holographic Human Transformation Theory is change on an Identity Level Change. The Transformation Theory consists of four aspects: Open and Closed Systems, Entropy, Totalities (Wholeness principle), and Quantum Leaps. The Physics of Correspondence is nature's way by which all of life works. These are five separate books with Workbooks, assignments and experiential techniques for learning to consciously work with the subconscious and its different organs and systems, based upon their individual functions and intelligence.

Holographic Human Transformation Theory consists of other books and other wisdom from the ancients, physics, and the scriptures.

Correspondence happens in the between anything. The Spirit resides in the between. Correspondence happens through the Spirit. The Spirit is the Substance of Correspondence.

Wholeness is the Unifying Force which holds us together. Inner Unification comes from the Macro-System to live and to grow. This is the background for the saying, "What we resist, persists." A Totality (Wholeness) is the state of being complete, entirety, Wholeness.

Correspondence governs function (purpose of action) and is the agreement of things with one another within the system to maintain the systems original purpose and function. When things are not corresponding, they become dysfunctional. Through correspondence all things function properly based upon their original purpose. Correspondence is the way things communicate between elements of itself and its environment. Correspondence isn't just communication. It is an agreement of the structure, patterns, and processes, the nature of communication between similar things.

The organs within our body must communicate with each other, family members must communicate with each other, and work settings must communicate. Correspondence is the Physics of Communication. A keyway of attaining greater correspondence and being more Open, is to create ways to increase the flow of information throughout the (your) entire system. In this book, I will explain in detail ways to create greater correspondence and provide guided meditations and experiential techniques. I hope you enjoy this Technology.

# CHAPTER 1
# PHYSICS LAWS OF CORRESPONDENCE

Correspondence is the way things communicate between elements of itself and its environment. Without correspondence between all things with any similarities there is deterioration. Intelligence is not the things that we know, it's the way that we have of knowing things applies to correspondence. If we know one thing, we know its opposite, and if we know one thing and observe a thing with similarities to the one thing we know, we know the other "similarities" as well. Correspondence isn't just communication. It is an agreement of the structure, patterns, and processes, the nature of communication between similar things.

The organs within our body must communicate with each other, family members must communicate with each other, and work settings must communicate. Correspondence is the Physics of Communication. There are structures, patterns, and processes in the physics of communication which are illustrated and dialogued. We can learn to implement these. Correspondence, as a Totality consists of three separate Elements working together with different purposes to create the correspondence as a Totality within the system. The three Elements of Correspondence are First) Similar, Second) Unity and Third) Integrate. As they pertain to the human senses, Sound and Sight are with the element of Similar, Touch and Energy are with the element of Unity and Taste and Smell are with the element of Integrate.

Correspondence governs Function; Function is the original purpose of anything in existence; everything has a function within it. Correspondence is the agreement of things with one another within the system to maintain the systems original purpose and function. When things are not corresponding, they become dysfunctional. Through correspondence all things function properly based upon their original purpose. Correspondence assures the original purpose of the system continues in its nature regardless of what happens within it or around it. Correspondence is very simple when it is taken in by the three Elements of correspondence. When elements are not corresponding, they system/totality does not function as it is originally intended to function. Elements of any Totality are simply the action, the identity, and the function of its contents, these are the complete ingredients of the identified Totality or whole. Anything that is a totality or an identified whole, just is. Everything intended for it to be total or whole is already within it. The action of the totality is the first element of any given totality, these are from thoughts and come from our past, our sense of sound and our sense of sight, our sense of sound quantum associated with the sense of right and our sense of sight quantum represented by our sense of wrong. The identity of a totality is the second element through which the totality exists. The identity element of the totality is present and emotion and associated with the sense of touch and energy. The sense of touch is quantum represented by the identity of God and the sense of energy quantum represented by the identity of self. The third element of any totality or whole being the actual function of it's contents. Actual function of contents being associated with the sense of taste and the sense of smell. The sense of taste being quantum associated with the function of purpose of life and the sense of smell quantum associated with the function of purpose of death. These are the nature, the structure, patterns and processes of any totality or whole. These are the elements of the existence.

Regarding Correspondence, its three Elements consists first of similar, then unity then integrate. Anything within the system that has similarities with any other parts, aspect ingredients of the same given system is the first element of the system being able to correspond. Everything corresponds based first upon Similar, second upon unity (deviations) and third upon integrate. Ingredients of identified totality consists of action, identity, function of contents, whatever any system is, we as an individual, is a whole system, family is a whole system, nature, time, wisdom, choice, there are many whole systems that are referred to as Totalities. Each Totality consists of 3 separate Elements and each of these 3 separate Elements Correspond through correspondence Elements of, first Similar, second Unity (deviations) and third Integrate.

Any whole system has different parts within the system, with separate purpose in the system for the function of the whole system. Every part within the whole system has particular similarities with other parts within the system. A relation between the parts, in which, each member of one set is associated with one or more members of the other, must exist for the system to accomplish its Function (purpose). Correspondence between the different parts of the whole system completes the systems Function. Communicating information within any given system, whether man made, or God made, is the Physics of Correspondence. What part of the airplane flies? Or what part of the car runs the car? It is the relationship, correspondence, and unifying wholeness that let the airplane fly, the car operate, and humans' function properly. Each whole system communicates by nature through the physics of correspondence. Correspondence, the action of the system due to the systems identity are the function of the contents within system as a whole.

Take the Totality of Time and Time's three Elements that make Time a whole and total system. Time consists of: First, past time, action of time. Second, present time, identity of time. Third, future time, function of contents of time. In order for Time as a Totality, a whole to function properly it must correspond, based upon the three elements of correspondence in the order of first element with the first Element of any other whole system, Totality and second element with the Totality of another given system's second Element and third Element of correspondence with the third Element of any other given totality's third Element. Totalities are whole systems already to function as a whole system they naturally correspond as a whole system. This always applies in this sequence for any of the elements there are three elements per each Totality, (first, second and then third element per each Totality). First element aligns with the first element of all other first elements. Second element aligns with second element of all other totalities and third element aligns with the third element of all other totalities.

Take the elements of Time, Family, Choice, and Correspondence. Put the elements from each totality sequentially with the associated element of another totality. It comes out like this: first elements associated: Past, Father, Take action, Action, Similar: second elements associated: Present, Mother, No Action, Identity, Unity; third elements associated: Future, Child, Let others take action, function of contents, Integrate.

Another Law governing Totality's and their Elements is this: if you can attain the third Element of any given totality, you automatically have the Totality (the Whole). The function of the contents of any totality or whole system is the functioning whole. Integrating the function of the systems contents into the original system is correspondence by the wholeness principle and totality.

A keyway of attaining greater correspondence and being more Open, is to create ways to increase the flow of information throughout the entire system, Communication. Whether this system is you as an individual, or a group, correspondence is the key factor in keeping the system whole. Without correspondence any system becomes dysfunctional and deteriorates as a whole system. Correspondence is by nature, a natural function within any system, based upon the function of the system as a whole system and the different functions of different aspects of parts within the system. Correspondence just is and just does based upon these three elements of correspondence. Correspondence is first the identity

Humans, as individuals are created to self-organize, to have unity, correspondence, and similarities. This is already within us, waiting to be drawn out. When these do not listen and respond to each other, there is deterioration. This happens on an individual basis, as well as in families, communities, countries, and the world. You can take conscious control and know these elements and make them a part of your system to keep the system properly functioning. Correspondence begins with aligning similarities within the system any deviations with the system must be unified, based upon their functions into the systems function (purpose). Unifying deviating parts of any systems consists of integrating these deviations into the system as a whole system. Deviations within the system are a functioning aspect of the system, assuring the systems growth. Every whole system has its function, its purpose and its potential for growth, correspondence is the physics for communicating within the system for the systems growth to greater potential. Correspondence consists of first similarities/actions, second deviations/identity and third integrating/function of contents of the whole.

# Chapter 2

# FUNCTION "OF" ORIGIN AND PURPOSE

Function is the action for which a thing exists, any action of a group of related actions is contributing to a larger action. Everything has a function for which it exists or the reason it has been made. This is also true regarding our life's experiences, they happen for a reason, they serve a purpose and there is a function they serve. When we have problems regarding our life's problems, we are fighting the function the problems serve instead of accepting the function of the problem.

Systemic; Relating to or consisting of a system, formulated as a coherent body of ideas, elements or principles. Systemic is methodical in its procedure, plan or approach. Systemic indicates an orderly pattern and its antonym is Disorderly. Systemic indicates careful, conscientious, painstaking, attention and the antonym is careless. The fact is that each part of the system corresponding together makes the system whole and the whole is greater than any one part. Each aspect, or element of any system has a function and purpose to the system, as a whole and correspondence is the physics of the system being whole.

Correspondence is the quantum physics of the system being a total, whole, in and of itself. Somewhat like "artificial intelligence", it just is. The three elements of totality are: first; action, second; identity, and third; function of contents of the totality. Take the three Elements of correspondence and totality: first: similar/action, second: unity/identity (deviations) and third: integrate/function of contents. Now take the three elements of choice, combine the elements of correspondence/totality with the elements of choice and see what happens? First element of choice: "Take Action" and combine it with first element of correspondence/totality, Similar/action "Take similar/action/action". Second element of choice "Take no action", combine with second element of correspondence/totality: unity/(deviations)/identity with "Taking no action", taking no action is unifying deviations for identity of the totality. Third element of Choice is "Let others take action" combine with third element of correspondence/totality; integrate/function of contents of totality. Let others take action to integrate the whole system and the function of the contents of the totality. Combine as to the function of the whole, individual deviations within the system.

## ALGORITHIM

The following Algorithm is based upon the totalities of Choice, and Correspondence and Totality and their Elements.

First element: take action, similar; take no action, similarity, take action, similar; let other's take action, integrate, take action, similar.

Second Element: take action, similar, take no action, unity; take no action, unity; let others take action, integrate, take no action, unity.

Third element: take action, similar, let others take action, integrate; take no action, let others take action, integrate; let others take action, integrate.

Take any given Whole (Totality), combine its elements through the elements of correspondence and the elements just naturally work together by their very nature. To correspond elements Wayne Schumaker created a continuum into an algorithm pattern from the totality of any given system. To make the algorithm Wayne took one element in each given set/system (totality) and added the one element to the other elements within that same or another set, in order to give continuum of the algorithm. This pattern also has a sequence of first element, then second element and then third element to the other elements within the same or another systems elements.

A mathematical correspondence assigns exactly one element of one set, to each element of the same, or another set. A variable as a quality, trait, or measurement, that depends on and varies with another. Result: Function implies a definite and or purpose that the one in question serves or a particular kind of work it is intended to perform. Procedure is to act in a particular manner. Behave, operate, work, go, run, and operate. Mathematical correlation between sets for the Whole creates the Function of the Whole (Totality).

Algorithm is a procedure for solving a mathematical problem in a finite number of steps that frequently involved repetition of an operation. An algorithm is a step-by-step procedure for solving a problem or accomplishing some end, an explicit set of rules for solving a problem.

A Continuum works with the algorithm process for correspondence in quantum physics as a mathematical measurement of quality and trait of elements of function within any given system. A mathematical correspondence assigns exactly one element of one set, to each element of the same, or another set. A variable as a quality, trait, or measurement, that depends on and varies with another. This mathematical process creates a pattern of consistency between the different elements along the continuum.

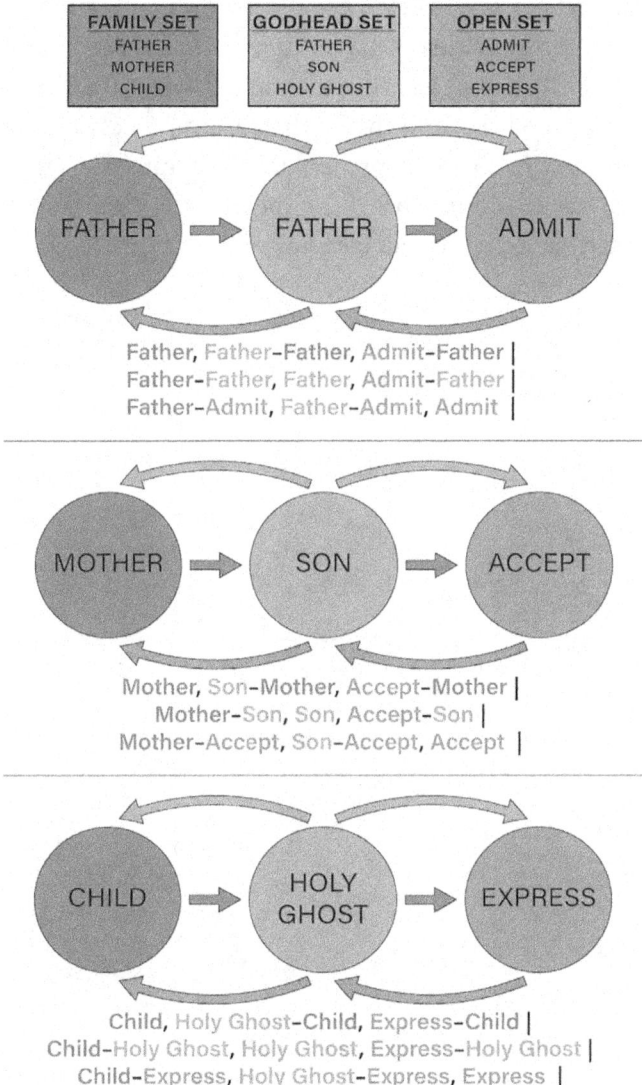

This process is adding the first element of a given set/system to the other elements of the same or similar set and the second element to the other elements and the third element to the other elements in the same or given system. This is the mathematical way of measuring between the different set/system, based upon the different set/systems different elements of data.

The mathematical algorithms are created based upon the data within the different whole systems. The data is communicating based upon the physics of correspondence, based upon first Element Similar, second Element Unity (deviation) and third Element Integration. Every individual element/data created through the mathematical process must correspond with one another in order to process the data into the system, thereby changing the systems Function of the Elements. Altering the function of the elements by adding another element to its character trait.

CHAPTER 3

# MATHEMATICS OF FUNCTION

Physics is a science that deals with matter and energy and their interactions. Physics is the nature of the physical processes and phenomena of a particular system and their physical properties and compositions. This is a Natural Science. Integration is the process of Unity (Deviations to Multiplicand); Act or process of integrating, to find the integral as of a function to incorporate into a larger unit. Forming, coordinating or blending elements into a functioning or unified whole. Integration is to incorporate parts of a system that are deviating from the other parts of the same system. Integrate is to combine as to the function of the whole, individual deviations within the system. Integration is the operation of finding a function whose differential is known, the operation of solving a differential equation (an equation containing differentials or derivatives of functions-compare PARTIAL DIFFERENTIAL EQUATION). Antonym is differentiation. What purpose/function does the antonym/differential/difference/deviation serve for the whole system? Deviation is a natural part of any given system. Systems are intended to progress, to grow, develop and change. Everything the system needs to maintain a natural growth process is within the system from the system's origin. Just as the idea, contains everything to attain the goal.

This also relates to the fact that Outcome is just one element of any given "Event", the other three Elements of the totality of Event are State and Condition and Outcome. You have to be in the right State and Condition to attain the Outcome. Even if you get the Outcome and you do not maintain or change the State or Condition for the Outcome, you can lose the Outcome. Yes. I know that you knew this and now you know it is a physics principle.

Let's take the Event system and do the Mathematical algorithm with its Antonyms; its deviations from the Event itself. Take each element and add it to the other elements in the same or another system.

Algorithm of Event

State, condition State, outcome State, state Condition, Condition, outcome Condition, state Integrate, condition Integrate, Integrate (add this to Correspondence System elements of Similar, Unity and Integrate). Similar, unity Similar, integrate Similar, similar Unity, Unity, integrate Unity, similar Integrate, unity Integrate, Integrate.

Event has a Purpose, an Origin and Function, this is it's beginning and the Fulfilling Phase when the Outcome of the Event is achieved. Not all Events even reach their Outcome, let alone begin and end without Deviation/differentials/antonyms. The prior identified pattern is the Mathematical measurements between the 2 separate Totality's (sets/systems/Multiplicand) and their Elements (Events and Correspondence). The Multiplicand being referred to in this process is the origin, the Forming phase, Idea phase. The Multiplicand is where the Purpose and Function of the whole system is.

We have different ways of referencing this principle of "getting off track", there is no "off track". This is another term for deviation, antonyms, differentials; these are all still parts of the Multiplicand and Purpose from the Forming, Beginning Phase and are intended to progress and evolve the Purpose. The mathematical pattern for the elements will inter-relate, inter-dependently any elements into the other systems. Placing these elements in this pattern increases the Function of each totality. So, as in the case of the Event Totality, any deviations that could have appeared to have been attempting to interfere with the Outcome are included to improve the Outcome of the Event.

Inherent sense of Right and Wrong by our Nature; Perhaps we can blame Adam and Eve and the damn apple. We are all spiritual beings, having a mortal experience. We have a constant sense knowing "Right from Wrong" it is inborn in our being. A Right being hard or difficult doesn't mean we don't know it is right. Many Right's are difficult to do. "Doing things right and Doing right things" can be opposite ways of doings. Things society, family, and other systems teach as Right is truly Wrong. We know the difference within us, an individual doing wrong on the basis of government or any other system knows they are doing wrong. Doing Right need not make a person a hero. Doing Right is God given to each individual as an inner sense and knowing (try it).

Correspondence occurs dimensionally by Direction, Questioning, and Modeling. These elements are the elements of the totality of Change:

Direction: As Human Beings we get this based upon our Past and based upon our Senses of SOUND and SIGHT. Guidance or supervision; Explicit instruction; Line or course on which something is moving or is aimed to move or along which something is pointing or facing. A channel, direct course of thought to action, of thought and effort.

Antonym: misdirection

Questioning: Human Beings base this Function on their Present and based upon our Senses of TOUCH and ENERGY. To ask a question of or about; Doubt, Dispute, to subject to analysis. Inquire; Alertly interested in finding out about things. Curious; inquisitive, inquiring searching. Antonym: incurious.

Modeling: Human Beings get this based upon the Future and upon the Senses of TASTE and SMELL. This aspect of Correspondence is to plan or form after a pattern into a shape to make into a system or whole. Produce a representation or simulation of display by using, designing or imitate a pattern. Antonym: Coincidence.

Permutation is change in character or condition, re-arranging existent Elements. Permutation is also the third Element of Transformation. Systems law states that if you have the third element of any given totality, you have the whole totality. Transformation as a totality consists of the three elements; Delete, Insert and Permutate. Transformation is Identity level change and Identity level change is change in Function for Purpose.

Changing by act or process; (lineal order) character or condition, Identity Level change of our Being applies to the dimensional map of the Holographic Human. Integrate (Integrity) based upon Structure, Patterns and Processes (of Natural Systems). (Dimensional HH Map of Elements Inter-related), work unified in a parallel Nature, (Natural, True Self Function), Elements Interrelated.

Similarity: Correspondence governs this (Process and Structure); Characteristics strictly comparable, this is adding and Inserting into the Whole System.

Unity: Conditions or Processes, Actions, Events, based upon the Multiplicand of Purpose of Totality.

Integrity: Structures and Processes unite to work in Parallels based upon Similarities. Similar parts Process Governs Function.

Integration of Concepts, Principles, Models and Programs already Interrelated and Interdependent in Parallel.

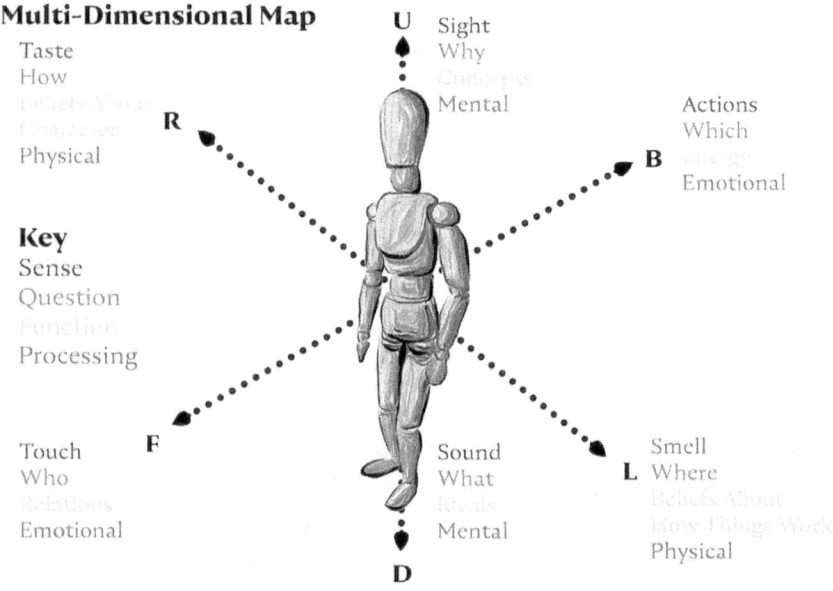

Similarity: Correspondence governs this (Process and Structure); Characteristics strictly comparable, this is adding and Inserting into the Whole System.

Unity: Conditions or Processes, Actions, Events, based upon the Multiplicand of Purpose of Totality.

Integrity: Structures and Processes unite to work in Parallels based upon Similarities. Similar parts Process Governs Function.

Integration of Concepts, Principles, Models and Programs already Interrelated and Interdependent in Parallel.

Function is the purpose of action for which something exists.

Mathematically assigning one Element of one set to each Element of the same set or another set, (a variable as a quality, trait or measurement that depends on or varies with another Elements, Contents), creates the change in character and condition.

Relationship of Elements, CONTENTS, is Correspondence between Function and Operation (Process). Unity of Deviation, Dissimilar of Structure and Patterns….Action for Deviating Structure or Process may be taken by an Event, Condition or Process (x the Purpose/Totality).

Event, an observed physical reality represented by a point designated by three coordinates of Place and one of Time.

Condition is a premise upon which the fulfillment depends; the Event is determined by the Condition. Changing Condition can put the Event into a State so an Action or Event Associated with one becomes associated with another; (Unity). Parallel; Change, Condition by "Raising" or doing something additionally.

Process is the Integrating to generate automatic response, (Program, Model).

(Bifurcation): a crossover point, serves purposes of change or growth in any given system. The point at which the system may begin to branch off is important, as it pertains to going on its own while taking the system with it.

Physics Laws Processes

Correspondence governs Function. Different Elements correspond through different processes.

Similarities expand times (Bifurcation Point) A point of branching off to another path so to speak.

Unity; deviations: Even deviating anomalies can correspond together. This is where the multiplicand comes into the process. The multiplicand is the original purpose of it all. Everything has a purpose; everyone has a purpose. When deviating anomalies appear remember the original purpose and multiply events and number of repetitions of the event of the purpose to the deviating anomaly.

Integration: Crossover Point; Crossover Point is Where the Bifurcation Point branches off to. In this process do not try to transform the bifurcation point to become to crossover point, allow both points to maintain their own identity. Just branch off to increase the system's ability to continue to grow with all it has learned.

# Chapter 4

## ELEMENTS OF CORRESPONDENCE

Totalities and Elements for Correspondence (Communication).

Totalities:

A) Human System
B) Wisdom
C) Body System Matrix
D) Nature
E) Success
F) Open System
G) Data Processing
H) Meta Programs
I) Communicate
J) Message
K) Dimension
L) Transformation

1) Mind/Mental, Perception

    a. Identity/Personality
    b. Data
    c. Models
    d. Structure
    e. Form
    f. Admit

g. Reception
   h. Data Processing
   i. Transmit
   j. Intent
   k. Height
   l. Delete

2) Emotions

   a. Communication; information processing and storage.
   b. Information; Dialogue, New theories, with Patterns.
   c. Processes
   d. Patterns; Natural or chance configuration, dissemble coherent system based on the intended interrelated workings of component parts.
   e. Norm
   f. Accept
   g. Storage
   h. Information Patterns and Storage.
   i. Receive
   j. Context
   k. Lateral
   l. Insert

3) Body, Understand, Discern

   a. Creation
   b. Knowledge; application, productive use of information and New Theories for Self and others
   c. Belief (Worldview).
   d. Processes; to Natural change.
   e. Fulfill, through integrative difference and modifications into the original patterns.
   f. Express
   g. Transmit
   h. Compressing for Models

i. Message
j. Content
k. Depth
l. Permutate

The Principle of Correspondence is the Union of Similar Parts. The Principle of Unity is the union of parts that are Dissimilar. Correspondence and Unity makes this work.

Reality Principle; is not knowing the difference of present, past or a vivid imagined experience.

Reality principle for the person with six senses: Resources are implied and not talked about in the Reality principle, (Do Right Things). The body teaches the mind about the resources. Sometimes other things need to be addressed first in the Reality principle, (Remembering Right). So, what it is they would prefer as their reality doesn't just change because of a thing they do. If the Reality principle isn't working, then they need to do something first before that reality can occur. Our not knowing the difference between present, past, future, or a vivid imagined experience makes the reality principal work. The law of correspondence and unity makes reality work.

Synergy: The whole is greater than the sum of its parts. This is speaking of the system where each part does what it is intended to do and communicates based upon Correspondence between the parts.

Incremental Change: Making small shifts in different human behaviors can be endless.

❖ Success Pattern, exploring possibilities for patterns or systems for change.
❖ Extend and improve the patterns and system for change.
❖ The System reached its potential and also shows it's built-in problems again. (Anomalies).

Transformative and Unpredictable Change: Identity Level Change.

- ❖ Success Pattern, exploring possibilities for patterns or systems for change.
- ❖ Extend and improve the patterns and the system for change.
- ❖ Success patterns considering anomalies.

Human beings have characteristics and attributes representative of sympathies, frailties, strengths and by nature of their minds can process and evaluate their lives and many other things. They have a conscious existence and may perceive and conceive other things into a real existence. Humans, by their very nature have transformed their actions and processes, not only of our world, even DNA of many other living things.

In order to transform, the key for the formula affecting Transformation is FUNCTION. Function is a literal operation that converts one thing into another: By deleting (removing from), inserting (adding to), or permutation (completely rearranging). Genetic modification happens this same way, by deleting, inserting, or permutation of DNA from one cell to another cell. This Physics of Transformation applies to human beings as well. Correspondence is the law governing this process of FUNCTION. Function indicates Purpose/Origin.

Integration is a process of unifying (unity), (Deviations to the Multiplicand Function). Humans transform and Integrate by nature, through their inherent sense of right and wrong. In accordance with and determined by their very nature, their structures, patterns and processes, inherently knowing Right and Wrong. The verb to integrate refers to the process of making whole or becoming whole.

Permutation is a major or fundamental change as in character or condition based primarily on the rearrangement of existent elements. Changing, by act or process, the lineal order of an ordered set or rearrangements of character or conditions.

Integrity exists because the Structure and Processes of Natural Systems are unified in ways that cause parts to work together in Parallel, through

Similarities and Correspondence. (Natural, True Self Function). Unity is based on the Universal law called; Oneness a totality of related parts: an entity that is a complete or systematic whole (Elements Interrelated). Integrity is a natural part of being human.

Law of similarity: The quality or state of being similar, correspondence is the Natural Law governing this Process. Alike in Substance or Essentials, Structure, Processes, and having characteristics in common (Co-strictly comparable, Isomorphic, Homeomorphism, to expand upon). This is where the Matrix Model comes into Transformation Theory. Taking Similar Correspondences and Unifying them to be One by adding (inserting) them into the Whole System. All things which are part of a whole system are having pieces that are similar to other pieces of the whole system. Correspondence helps these different parts of the whole system function together for the systems purpose.

Integration of Concepts, Principles, Models, and Programs already Interrelated and Interdependent in Parallel.

Unity of Conditions or Processes, Actions, Events based upon the Multiplicand of Purpose or Totality. Similar parts process governs Function.

Correspondence occurs dimensionally by Direction, Questioning and Modeling.

Integration of Concepts and Principles, Models and Programs must be Interrelated and Interdependent.

Correspondence is the Parts or Processes of the same shape or form resonating as one.

Unity is the Continuity of Deviations without Deviation or change as in Purpose of the Actions, Events, Conditions or Processes. These are to be based upon the Multiplicand (Original Purpose) or the Totality (Wholeness Principle).

# Chapter 5

# FUNCTION: PURPOSE OF ACTION FOR WHICH SOMETHING EXISTS

Correspondence governs Function; Function is the original purpose of anything in existence; everything has a function within it. Correspondence is the agreement of things with one another within the system to maintain the system's original purpose and function. When things are not corresponding, they become dysfunctional. Dysfunction is a result of Origin, Purpose, Process, deviating from itself; another way is to say when you are off track.

Mathematically assign one Element of one set to Each Element of the same or another set: A variable as a quality, trait or measurement that depends on or varies with another.

Integrity: Structures and Processes of Natural Systems unite to work in Parallel, based on Similarities and Correspondence.

Law of correspondence; A particular similarity. A relation between sets in which each member of one set is associated with one or more members of the other. To correspond means to respond together, to react in unison at the same time. Nature streamlines systems by having parts or processes with the same shape or form to resonate as one. Principle of correspondence is the union of similar parts. This process of Correspondence of similar parts or processes unifying Governs Function. Changing Function causes

Transformation. Correspondence occurs dimensionally by direction, questioning, and modeling. Similar parts change together.

Function represents "Purpose" of an action specifically fitted or used or for which something exists. Groups of Elements or related actions contributing to a larger action. A Mathematical correspondence that assigns exactly one Element of one set to each Element of the same or another set. A variable (as a quality, trait, or measurement) that depends on and varies with another. Function relates to performance. Correspondence governs Function.

The word "Of" is used to represent Function. "Of" indicates the Component Material, Parts or Elements or Contents. "Of" as a Function word indicates a part or point of Reckoning, Origin or Derivation, as well as a Cause, Motivator or Reason. The word "Of" is used to indicate a whole or quantity from which a Part is Removed (Deleted) or Expanded (Inserted) or Rearranged (Permutated), to indicate Relationships (Correspondence) between a result determined by a Function or Operation (Process) and a basic entity (as an independent variable), to indicate characteristic or distinctive possessions or possession in Time. Other ways of using the word "Of", indicating Function: As, for, as to, on, upon, concerning, pertaining.

Three aspects of being Human which correspond are: Mind, Emotion, and Body.

TOTALITY; NATURAL BEING (Higher Levels of Human System Function)

1. Identity, Personality, Mind

2. Communication and Information Processing, Emotional Functions

3. Creation, Behavioral, Body

Each higher level of human functions has the ability of thinking for each of the human functions. The human senses are included in this thinking process. Much of this thinking is done automatically by the subconscious on the TDS through what are known as Meta programs.

The Unity principle or law: A totality of related parts, an entity that is a complex or systematic whole. Unifying aspects of Naturally Integrating Systems. A quality or state of being One, not multiple, One Identity. This aspect of Unity is Continuity without deviation or change as in Purpose of Actions. Any deviation or change is to be taken back to Purpose and multiplied by Purpose.

The Union of parts that are Dissimilar: Structures and Processing's which Deviate from one another in the same System. Action for Deviating Structure or Process may be taken by an Event, Condition or Process multiplied into Purpose and/or Totality.

Event: The Fundamental entity of observed physical reality represented by a point designated by 3 coordinates of Place and 1 of Time in the Space-Time Continuum postulated by the Theory of Relativity. Events are Outcomes, something that happens, the fundamental entity observable with a physical reality, events are done to achieve an end.

Relativity (A quality or state of being relative): Something that is Relative. The state of being dependent for existence on or determine in Nature, Value, or Quality by relation to something else. A thing based on the 2 postulates. 1. That the speed of light in a vacuum is constant and independent of the source or observed. 2. That the mathematical forms of the laws of physics are invariant in all inertial systems and which leads to the assertion of the equal of mass and energy and of change in mass, dimension, and time with increased velocity.

## Higher Level of Human Function Algorithm

Directions: Please read this algorithm as it is written out. This may be read by one's self or, delivered in a group setting by an instructor. Remember, an algorithm is a step-by-step procedure for solving a problem or accomplishing some end, an explicit set of rules for solving a problem. It is often beneficial to write about your experience following this exercise. Enjoy.

There are levels of function having the ability to think for each of the other levels of human function.

These levels having this ability are:

First: Identity

Second: Communication

Third: Creation

Each of these are higher level totalities and as such each of these totalities have three different elements. These three different elements must correspond with one another in order to function properly. Elements correspond with one another through algorithms. Algorithms assist the different elements to interact-interdependently. Simply by reading and thinking about these algorithms can assist the subconscious and the conscious to focus on the potential of our human levels of function.

First decide and focus on a great identity of yourself. This identity can be anything you choose it to be. Create in your mind or imagine an incredible you with wonderful traits and knowledge, with great wisdoms and discernments. Create or imagine to create an Identity of you with great success, with wisdom and awareness to learn from and grow easily from any of life's challenges. A strong in mind, emotion and ability to create whatever you decide. An identity of you such as you may never have even dared to image before, create this identity of you now and nod your head when you have pictured or imagined this identity of this incredible successful you.

(Wait a moment depending on the size of the group and then say "Thank you")

Identity

Focus on this identity of you, as you have created or imagined it in your mind. This incredible identity of self. Your identity with wonderful traits, knowledge, great wisdoms, success, awareness of learning and growth from any, and all of life's challenges. Focus on this Identity of you as you, picture you as this identity. Thank you. Now, please… focus on the personality of this identity of you. The personality of this identity of you.

(Pause a moment)

Now, if you would please focus…. on the Mind of this identity of you. The mind of this identity of you with wonderful traits, knowledge, great wisdoms, success, awareness of learning and growing from any, and all of life's challenge. Focus on the thoughts, the thinking processes of the mind of this identity of you.

(Pause a moment)

Now focus on this identity's personality, just the identity of you with this identity's personality. Now just focus on your personality as this identity. Your personality as incredible with wonderful traits, with knowledge, great wisdoms, success, awareness of learning and growth from any, and all of life's challenges. Thank you. Now, if you would please, focus on the mind of this identity of you and focus also upon the personality of the mind of this incredible identity of self. Your identity with wonderful traits, knowledge, great wisdoms, success, awareness of learning and growth from any, and all of life's challenges. Thank you.

(Pause a moment)

Communication

Communication. Focus on the communication of this identity of you with great success, with wisdom and awareness to learn from and grow easily from any of life's challenges. A strong in mind, emotion and ability to create whatever you decide. An identity of you such as you may never have even dared to image before, create this identity of you now and nod your head when you have pictured or imagined this identity of this incredible successful you. Focus on the communication of this you. Thank you.

Now, if you would please, focus of the information processing of this identity of you with this identity's communications. The process for the communication of this identities communicating, its information processing. Thank you.

Now, focus on the emotion function of this identity of you with great success, with wisdom and awareness to learn from and grow easily from any of life's challenges. A strong in mind, emotion and ability to create whatever you decide. Focus on or imagine the emotion function of this identity's way of communicating its information processing. Thank you.

Now, if you would please, focus on the communication-information processing of this identity of you. Now if you would please just focus on identities information processing, just its information processing for its communications. Now focus on this identity's emotion function and the information processing of this emotion function for this identity of you. Thank you.

Now, if you would please, focus on the communication of this identity of you and the emotion function of the communication of this identity of you. Now focus on the information processing of this identity of you and focus on the emotion function of this information processing of this identity of you. Thank you. Now, please, focus on just the emotion function of this identity of you.

(Pause a moment)

Creation

Focus now on the creations this identity of you can do. This identity of you with wonderful traits and knowledge, with great wisdoms and discernments. You with great success, with wisdom and awareness to learn from and grow easily from any of life's challenges. A strong in mind, emotion and ability to create whatever you decide. An identity of you such as you may never have even dared to image before. Focus now on all this identity of you can create. Thank you. Now, please focus on the behaviors of the actual creations this identity can create for you. Thank you. Now, please, focus on the body of the creations this identity can create for you. Focus on the bodies of these creations this identity can create for you. Now, if you would please, focus on the creation of this identity of you and focus on this identity's creational behaviors. Thank you. Focus on the body of this identity of the creations of you and focus on the body's behaviors. Now, focus on the creation of this identity of you and its body. Thank you. Now, focus on the behaviors of the bodies of this creation of this identity of you. Now, please just focus on the body of the creations of this identity of you. This you with wonderful traits and knowledge, with great wisdoms and discernments. You with great success, with wisdom and awareness to learn from and grow easily from any of life's challenges. A strong in mind, emotion and ability to create whatever you decide. An identity of you such as you may never have even dared to image before. Thank you.

# Chapter 6

# GRAVITATION AND RELATED ACCELERATION PHENOMENA

Space/Time Continuum: A coherent Whole, characterized as a collection, sequence or progression of Values, or Elements, varying by minute degrees. "Good and Bad stand at opposite ends of a Continuum instead of describing the 2 halves of a line" (Wayne Shumaker). The set of Real Numbers including both the rationales and the irrationals, a composite set which cannot be serrated into 2 sets. Neither of which contains a limit point of the other. A coherent Whole; boundless progression of values and elements varying by minute degrees. Gravitation does not exist in the dirt, road pavement, or rubber on tires. None of these things have gravitation to them, in them, nor about them. Gravitation is an interaction between objects. Space is a boundless 3-dimensional extent, in which objects, events, conditions, or processes occur and have Relative position and direction (infinite Space and Time).

Condition: A premise upon which the fulfillment depends. The Event itself is determined upon the Condition. Condition is essential to the appearance or occurrence of the Function of Purpose. Condition can restrict or modify the state of being of the Purpose. Changing Condition brings or puts the Event into a specific state; adapting and modifying, so an Action or Event associated with one becomes associated with another. Condition may be Raised or changed by doing something Additionally.

Process or "Process of Time": A Natural phenomenon marked by gradual changes that lead toward particular results. Continuing Natural Activity or Function with Actions conducing to an end. The prominent or projecting part of a living Structure, Integrating Sensory Data so Action (Automatic Response) is Generated.

Reality Principle: The reality principle works with unity and correspondence principle both consciously and subconsciously. Consciously, we create our own reality based on the things we perceive. We can also watch a movie or read a book and get sad or angry or frightened, even though it's just a book or a movie. Subconsciously, we don't know the difference between real and imagined, it just is.

Wholeness Principle: The wholeness principle is a unifying force in each of us that holds us together. Inner Unification come from the Macro-System to live and to grow. A natural desire for wholeness, unification, and wellness that comes from each living intelligent aspect of our being to be whole and healthy and a part with us. This is why, what we resist, persists. The unseen unifying force that promotes integration of all aspects of our being. This unifying force is of nature and based on our fundamental choice to live. It wants us to live, it wants to live as each individual cell, and so nature itself promotes integration of all our parts.

Synergy: Synergy is the whole greater than the individual parts and it applies to everything. The interactions of two or more agents for a whole. Whatever the whole is, there are three aspects that are individual to the whole. Systems working together are Synergetic. Systems are enmities or patterns that interact with each other for a process. The relationship between the parts is the fundamentals of its processes.

The conscious field is formed by a unifying force that is intelligent and aware. An individual's level of personal development can be measured by their ability to perceive the field in self and others, and the synergy of the whole based on the correspondence and unity of the individual parts together.

When the surrounding plummets, the center collapses, leaving us out of balance, or innocence. In no sense, don't recognize it, nor can we pick up on it in any sense. Here are a few examples and I am sure you can identify more; addiction, mental, emotional, and physical disease are signs of the collapse.

NATURE: Structures, Patterns, Processes

NATURE: The inherent character or basic constitution of a person or thing: A creative and controlling force in the universe. An inner force and the sum of such forces in an individual. A kind and class distinguished by fundamental and essential characteristics. The origin of the natural condition.

STRUCTURE: The action of building. Arranged in a definite pattern of organization. The arrangement of particles and parts into a substance or body. Organization of the parts as dominated by the general constitution and character of the whole. The aggregate of elements of an entity in their relationship to one another. "Of", relates to or being a method in which each step of the solution to the problem is contained in a separate sub-program.

PATTERN: A form or pattern proposed for imitation. A natural or chance configuration. A reliable sample of traits, acts, tendencies, and other observable characteristics. A discernible coherent system based on the intended interrelationship of component parts. Frequent or widespread incidences.

PROCESSES: To progress, advance, ongoing, and proceed. Natural phenomenon marked by gradual changes that lead toward a particular result with a continual natural or biological activity or Function. The prominent or projecting part of the structure which is subject to a special process. To subject or handle through an established routine set of procedures.

Matrix of Correspondence: MAP

Integration is the Process of "Unity" (Deviations to Multiplicand)

Correspondence Governs Function

# PHYSICS LAWS AND HOLOGRAPHIC HUMAN THEORY

Similarity: Expand

Unity: Taking deviating Anomalies and paralleling them to become more similar to be able to increase the ability within any given system.

Correspondence: Correspondence governs function. Nature having parts or processes at any level, of the same shape or form resonates as one. Similar parts change together. Example: Two electrons, when one changes its spin, the other one changes its spin also. The Totality of related parts that are in a complex whole naturally correspond and affect each other, leaving the Multiplicand unchanged.

The Human System IS A WHOLE SYSTEM and can unify parts that are very different!!!

Integration/Integrated Systems: Elements and Function are interrelated and interdependent upon other Elements and Function. Changing one Element of an Integrated System affects the rest of the system's entirety. Integration is the process of making Whole and this works due to Correspondence, Unity, Reality, and Wholeness Principles. There are 4 types of Integration Systems or Models: 1) Symbolic, 2) Energetic, 3) Whole Body, 4) Linguistic. Integrity is the condition of being whole or complete; to integrate is the process of making Whole. Integrity exists because the structure and processes of Natural Systems are Unified in a way that causes parts to work together in Parallel, Similarities and Correspondence.

Quantum Leaps and Unbridgeability

Unbridgeability is about choice. Unbridgeability is to be against, to be unaccepted, unabsorbed, unaccredited, and unacknowledged. Choice is a quantum leap syndrome. Quantum leap syndrome is a Matrix continuum of sets of elements placed in a Mathematical continuum.

Human beings are born with Quantums; 1 per each human sense:

Sound: Right - Sight: Wrong

Touch: God - Energy: Self

Taste: Life - Smell: Death

These Quantums are God-Given and never leave us here on Earth. No matter how hard we may try to numb or quiet them, they never calm down nor just go away.

We have an inner sense of all of these Quantums, and they constantly remind us of their, and our own purpose. When we accept these and listen to them, we are happy and more positive. When we try to ignore or conquer them, we struggle.

There are 3 different aspects regarding Choice: 1) Take Action, 2) Take no Action, 3) Let another Take Action. Choice being an option, alternative, preference, selection, and/or election. Be willing to let go to be self and God. Nurture self when others are not willing to choose to go with you, they choose to stay.

Resistance occurs when associated quantums aren't bridgeable. Bridging the quantums incorporates the physics of correspondence. The continuum of opposites and opposition by taking one element of each set and adding it to the other elements of the same or another set.

Bridging the Quantum's take you to a point of Transformation. When bridging the quantums, you bridge from the left side to the right side. Beginning from the top of the Map to the bottom of the Map. Combining Wrong with Right, Self with God, and Death with Life.

Quantum Leaps:

➢ Right and Wrong

Right: Conforming with or conformable to justice, law. Continue from above. Not spurious, genuine. Just, sound, legal, proper, toward, on the right, in a straight line. Being in accordance with what is just, good, or proper. Conforming to facts or truth.

Wrong: Not on conformity with fact or truth, incorrect or erroneous. In a wrong course, sometimes contrary to. An unjust or injurious act, to go astray or alter. Principles, practices, or conduct contrary to justice, goodness, equity, or law. Not right or proper according to a code, standard or convention.

➢ God and Self

God: The supreme or ultimate reality; the Being perfect in power, wisdom, and goodness who is worshipped as creator and ruler of the universe. A being or object believed to have more than natural attributes and powers and to require human worship, one controlling a particular aspect or part of reality.

Self: The total, essential, particular being of a person. The entire person of an individual, the realization or embodiment of an abstraction. An individual's typical character or behavior. The union of elements (as body, emotions, thoughts, and sensations) that constitute the individuality and identity of a person. Of the same character throughout, of the same material. Many words beginning with self have been added to the dictionary.

➢ Life and Death

Life: The property or quality that distinguishes living. To continue from above. A principle or force that is considered to underlie the distinctive quality of animate beings. The sequence of physical e process of living. A specific phase of earthly existence. The form or pattern of something existing in reality.

Death: The act of dying, termination of life. A permanent cessation of all vital functions. The cause or occasion of loss of life.

These synthesis with:

Sound; Right

Sight; Wrong

Touch; God

Energy; Self

Smell; Death

Taste; Life

The Quantum Leaps are a Continuum. A continuum is a coherent whole characterized as a collection, sequence, or progression of values or Elements varying by minute degrees. "Good and bad stand at opposite ends of a continuum instead of describing the two halves of a line" (Wayne Shumaker). The set of real numbers include both the rationales and the irrationals broadly; a compact set which cannot be separated into two sets. Neither of which contains a limit point of the other. It is continuous.

Mind: Right and Wrong

Emotion: God and Self

Body: Life and Death

Two quantum leaps each.

# Chapter 7

# HUMAN TRANSFORMATION THEORY

Human beings have characteristics and attributes representative of frailties, sympathies, strengths, and by nature of their minds can process and evaluate their lives and many other things. They have a conscious existence and may perceive and conceive other things into a real existence. Humans, by their very nature have transformed their actions and processes. Not only our world, even DNA of many other living things.

In order to transform, the key of the formula affecting Transformation is FUNCTION. Function is a literal operation that converts one thing into another (by deleting, inserting, or permutation). Genetic modification happens in a bacteria, by inserting of DNA from another bacteria cell. Permutation is the act or process of changing; rearranging the lineal order of, and ordered set of objects, and/or ordered arrangement of a set of elements. Permutation is fundamental change in character or condition, based primarily on rearrangement of existent elements (Mathematical Matrix).

Correspondence is the law governing this process of FUNCTION. Integration is a process of unifying (unity). Humans transform and Integrate by nature. Their inherent sense of right and wrong, in accordance with and determined by their very nature. Permutation is a major or fundamental change as in character or condition based primarily on the rearrangement of existent elements. Changing, by act or process, the lineal order of an ordered set or rearrangements of character or conditions.

Integrate refers to the process of making whole or becoming whole. Integrity exists because the Structure and Processes of Natural Systems are Unified in ways that cause parts to work together in Parallel, through Similarities and Correspondence (Natural, True Self Function). Unity is based on the Universal law, "Oneness", a totality of related parts; an entity that is a complete or systematic whole (Elements Interrelated).

Law of similarity: The quality or state of being similar. Correspondence is the Natural Law governing this Process. Alike in Substance or Essentials, Structure and Processes. Having characteristics in common, strictly comparable. Isomorphic, Homeomorphic, to expand upon. This is where the Matrix Model comes into Transformation Theory. Taking Similar Correspondences and Unifying them to be One by Adding (Inserting) them into the Whole System.

Integrity: Structures and Processes of Natural Systems unite to work in Parallel, based on Similarities and Correspondence. Integration, Concepts and Principles, Models and Programs Interrelated and Interdependent. Correspondence is the Parts or Processes of the same shape or form resonate as one. Unity is the Continuity of Deviations without Deviation or change as in Purpose of the Actions, Events, Conditions or Processes. These are to be based upon the Multiplicand, the Original Purpose or the Totality, Wholeness Principle.

Law of correspondence: A particular similarity, a relation between sets in which each member of one set is associated with one or more members of the other. To correspond means to respond together to react in unison at the same time. Nature streamlines systems by having parts or processes with the same shape or form to resonate as one. Principle of correspondence is the union of similar parts. This process of Correspondence of similar parts or processes unifying Governs Function and changing Function causes Transformation. Correspondence occurs dimensionally by direction, questioning, and modeling. Similar parts change together.

Function represents PURPOSE of an action specifically fitted or used or for which something exists (Groups of Elements or related actions contributing to a larger action). A Mathematical correspondence that assigns exactly one Element of one set to each Element of the same or another set. A variable (as a quality, trait, or measurement), that depends on and varies with another. Function relates to performance. Correspondence governs Function.

The word "Of", is used to represent Function, "Of" indicates the Component Material, Parts, Elements, or Contents. "Of" as a Function word indicates a part or point of Reckoning, Origin, or Derivation, as well as a Cause, Motivator, or Reason. The word "Of" is used to indicate a whole or quantity from which a Part is Removed (Deleted) or Expanded (Inserted) or Rearranged (Permutated), to indicate Relationships (Correspondence) between a result determined by a Function or Operation (Process) and a basic entity (as an independent variable), to indicate characteristic or distinctive possessions, possession in Time. Other ways of using the word "Of" indicating Function: as for, as, as to, on, upon, concerning, pertaining. Function is the original purpose of anything in existence; everything has a function within it. Correspondence is the agreement of things with one another within the system to maintain the system's original purpose and function. When things are not corresponding, they become dysfunctional. Through correspondence all things function properly based upon their original purpose. Dys-Function is a result of Origin, Purpose, Process, deviating from itself, another way is to say when you are off track. Deviate from one another in the same System. Action for Deviating Structure or Process may be taken by an Event, Condition, or Process, multiplied into Purpose and/or Totality.

Event: The Fundamental entity of observed physical reality represented by a point designated by 3 coordinates of Place and 1 of Time in the Space-Time Continuum postulated by the Theory of Relativity. Events are Outcomes, something that happens, the fundamental entity observable with a physical reality. Events are done to achieve an end.

Relativity: A quality or state of being relative. Something that is Relative. The state of being dependent for existence on or determine in Nature, Value, or Quality, by relation to something else. A thing based on the

2 postulates: 1. That the speed of light in a vacuum is constant and independent of the source or observed. 2. The mathematical forms of the laws of physics are invariant in all inertial systems and which leads to the assertion of the equalness of mass and energy and of change in mass, dimension, and time with increased velocity. An extension to the Theory to include gravitation and related acceleration phenomena.

Space/Time Continuum: A coherent Whole, characterized as a collection, sequence or progression of Values or Elements, varying by minute degrees. "Good and Bad stand at opposite ends of a Continuum instead of describing the 2 halves of a line" (Wayne Shumaker).

The set of Real Numbers including both the rationales and the irrationals, a composed set which cannot be serrated into 2 sets neither of which contains a limit point of the other. Space is a boundless 3-dimensional extent in which objects and events, conditions or processes occur and have Relative position and direction (infinite Space and Time).

Condition: A premise upon which the fulfillment depends. The Event itself is determined upon the Condition. Condition is essential to the appearance or occurrence of the Function of Purpose. Condition can restrict or modify the state of being of the Purpose. Changing Condition brings or puts the Event into a specific state; adapting and modifying, so an Action or Event associated with one becomes associated with another. Condition may be Raised or changed by doing something Additionally.

Process/Process of Time: A Natural phenomenon marked by gradual changes that lead toward particular results. Continuing Natural Activity or Function, leading Actions conducing to an end. Process is the prominent or projecting part of a living Structure then Integrating Sensory Data, so Action and Automatic Response is generated.

Correspondence governs Function; Function is the original purpose of anything in existence; everything has a function within it. Correspondence is the agreement of things with one another within the system to maintain the systems original purpose and function. When things are not corresponding, they become dysfunctional. Through correspondence all things function properly based upon their original purpose. Correspondence is the way things communicate between elements of itself and its environment. Without correspondence between all things with any similarities there is deterioration. Correspondence isn't just communication. It is an agreement of the structure, patterns, and processes, the nature of communication between similar things.

The organs within our body must communicate with each other, family members must communicate with each other, and work settings must communicate. Correspondence is the Physics of Communication. A keyway of attaining greater correspondence and being more Open, is to create ways to increase the flow of information throughout the entire system, Communication. Everything has a function for which it exists or the reason it has been made. This is also true regarding our life's experiences, they happen for a reason, they serve a purpose and there is a function they serve. When we have problems regarding our life's problems, we are fighting the function the problems serve instead of accepting the function of the problem. The fact is that each part of the system corresponding together makes the system whole and the whole is greater than any one part. Each aspect, or element of any system has a function and purpose to the system, as a whole and correspondence is the physics of the system being whole. Correspondence is the quantum physics of the system being a total, whole, in and of itself. Somewhat like "artificial intelligence", it just is. Take any given Whole (Totality), combine its elements through the elements of correspondence and the elements just naturally work together by their very nature. To correspond elements Wayne Schumaker created a continuum into an algorithm pattern from the totality of any given system. An algorithm is a procedure for solving a mathematical problem in a finite number of steps that frequently involved repetition of an operation. An algorithm is a step-by-step procedure for solving a problem or accomplishing some end, an explicit set of rules for solving a problem. A Continuum works with the algorithm process for correspondence in quantum physics as a mathematical measurement of quality and trait of elements of function within any given system. A mathematical correspondence assigns exactly one element of one set, to each element of the same, or another set. A variable as a quality, trait, or measurement, that depends on and varies with another. This mathematical process creates a pattern of consistency between the different elements along the continuum.

## QUANTUM QUESTIONING AND ALGORITHM

Directions: Identify and write down the challenge, opportunity, or goal you are working on. Then, simply answer the following questions using the 2 second rule. Then read through the algorithm of elements an odd number of times. Following this, it's often helpful to free write a response. In a group setting, the instructor will direct the participants to write down on paper the challenge, opportunity, or goal they are individually or collectively working on. The instructor will then ask the questions while the participants write down their answers using the 2 second rule. The instructor will then direct the participants to focus in on their own answers to the questions, while being open to the algorithm being read out loud by the instructor. Following this, the instructor will direct the participants to begin free writing a response to the experience.

NOTE: The comma indicates another totality or element, and a hyphen sign indicates an element added to another element and these are spoken with emphasis on their interrelating-interdependently. A / sign indicates a new algorithm set with the whole algorithm.

## QUANTUM QUESTIONING AND ALGORITHM (TECHNIQUE)

### Quantum Questioning

What am I frail about?

Why am I frail about these?

What is Right about my frailties?

Why might my frailties be Wrong?

What am I uncertain about related to my frailties? What ones are Right?

Why am I uncertain about these similar to the frailties? Why are some of these Wrong?

Who are my Sympathies about?

Who relates these with God?

Which is these Sympathies do I act upon or get intuition about?

Which of these are just of myself?

Who of my Sympathies relate presently with my Doubt and my doubt of God?

Which of my Sympathies and actions or intuitions is my present or current Doubt of or about?

Which are just of myself?

How will my limiting beliefs affect my life?

How do my limiting beliefs affect my death?

Where will my limiting beliefs strategize my death? And my life?

How will my strengths help my life? And my death?

Where will my strengths strategize my l life? And my death?

## Quantum Algorithms

What, why- What, when- What, What-why, why, when- why.

What- when, why- when, when, Who, which- who, when- who. Who- which, which, when-which, Who- when, which- when, when. How, where- how, when- how, how- where, when- where, how- when, where- when, when.

Right, Wrong- right, When- right. Right- wrong, Wrong, When- wrong. Right- when, Wrong- when, When.

God, Self-God, When-God. God- Self, Self, When- Self. God- when, Self- when, When.

Life, death-life, when-life. Life-death, death, when-death. Life-when, death-when, when.

# Chapter 8

# REALITY PRINCIPLE AND TRANSFORMATION

Reality Principle works with unity and correspondence principle both consciously and subconsciously. Consciously, we create our own reality based on the things we perceive. We can also watch a movie or read a book and get sad or angry or frightened, even though it's just a book or a movie. Subconsciously, we don't know the difference between real and imagined, it just is.

Wholeness Principle: There is a unifying force in each of us that holds us together, Inner Unification come from the Macro-System to live and to grow. A natural desire for wholeness, unification, wellness, that comes from each living, intelligent aspect of our being to be whole and healthy and a part with us. This is why what we resist, persists. A unifying force that promotes integration of all aspects of our being. This unifying force is of nature is based on our fundamental choice to live. It wants us to live and wants to live as each individual cell and so nature itself promotes integration of all our parts Synergy is this unified force as one, the whole greater than the individual parts, this applies to everything. The interactions of two or more agents for a whole. The whole being the purpose and function of the system and the reason for each part. Whatever the whole is, there are three aspects that are individual to the whole and each of these three aspects can have different parts within them. Systems working together are Synergetic. Systems are enmities or patterns that interact with each other for a process. The relationship between the parts is the fundamentals of its processes. The relationship between each part is Correspondence, the ultimate integration of each individual aspect of the whole into the greater function and purpose based upon each individual part's purpose and function.

The conscious field is formed by a unifying force that is intelligent and aware. An individual's level of personal development can be measured by their ability to perceive the field in self and others and the synergy of the whole based on the correspondence and unity of the individual parts together.

## TOTALITY TRANSFORMATION TECHNIQUE

Determine from the list of TOTALITIES, the specific 1 you will use for doing this technique. Write on 3 separate pieces of paper the (Elements) Functions of the Totality and place them on the ground in their order of 1, 2 and 3. They are listed in their proper order on the page listing the Totalities. Make sure to have space between each piece of paper to take one or two steps as you will walk from one to the other through this technique.

Stand, with space for 2 steps between yourself and the first (Element) Function on the ground.

"Now, imagine or pretend to imagine, placing your entire life's experiences between yourself and the first positioned (Element) Function on the ground." (Pause and watch them, giving them time to place this on the ground).

"Not, now, but in a moment, I'll instruct you to walk through your life's experiences and stand on the first (Element) Function placed on the ground, in front of you. When you arrive at the first Function you will stand there, with your eyes opened or closed, that's entirely up to you. I will guide you through the (Element) Function process for this first Function regarding your life's experience. Thank you, please walk through your life's experience now and stop on the first (Element) Function."

(Pause and give them a moment to do this).

"Not now, but in a moment, I will guide you through this first (Element) Function processes. These are Filters in the subconscious and this first filter is Perception, Identity and Personality. These are of your Past and you may now choose of yourself the Data from your life's experience for you to use to expand upon for your Personality, your Identity, of your choosing. The symbols, dates, sounds, sights, intuitions, textures, smells and tastes and energies. All of these in simple or complex symbols of your choosing, and placing these symbols into a internal structures of character traits, mental and emotional traits. Expanding and joining any symbols and representations of a similar basis. Taking symbols and all this Data, of your choosing and noticing any symbols of this for you which might deviate from the other symbols and imagine or pretend to imagine adjusting the Different symbols so they become more similar with each other, more similar with the collection of symbols as you have chosen. These are the filters of your Perception, for your Identity, for your Personality, as you choose to be. " (Focus your instructions including the Totality Functions they have laid on the ground into your dialogue of instructions to them as you guide them through each step in your dialogue.) (Pause and allow them some time to complete this process, you might repeat some of the instruction over to assist them in completing this first step.) (When they have completed this step be sure to thank them. Then continue with the technique instructions.)

"Now, please, taking all of the collection of symbols and senses and Data you have chosen to your Identity, Personality and Perceptions regarding all of your life's experience, imagine or pretend to imagine placing all of these on the ground in front of you, between yourself and the second Filter you have placed upon the ground. And after you have done this again, walking through all of this Data from your life's experience, walk through all of this and stand upon the second Filter placed upon the ground, in front of you." (Pause, giving them time to complete this process. Again, you may repeat the instructions and pause, giving them time to complete this. When they have done this and have walked through their life's experience and are standing on the second filter, continue with the dialogued instructions.)

"Thank you. Now, this Data you choose imagine, or pretend to imagine making models and different patterns of this Data and symbols. Create your own sentences, dialogues, information about these symbols and the Data. Unify and Integrate the Data into dialogue, sentences for internal information for you, they may naturally become dialogue and sentences and information, some might require your assistance in relating to some of the other models and patterns and you may imagine or pretend to imagine multiplying some with common symbols and dialogues of your choosing for your purpose for your life's experience. Noticing any deviations or anomalies and integrating these with common multiples to create your sentences, your dialogue for your information. For your internal processing for your present moments for your experiences. You're your dialogue and sentences of the Data create New Theories for your life's experience. New applications and productive use for you personally from the information. Creating meaningful patterns to use in each moment of your life, built upon your Life's New Theories, new applications for you to experience. Create communication patterns for these New theories and models, so they may interact and relate with one another and be in correspondence with your New Theories for your life's New experiences.

Rearranging any information you choose to in order to create any New Theories you may choose to create for your life's experiences." (Add in any other aspects pertaining to the specific Filtering process they have chosen and are standing on, dialogue this also into your instructions and guiding them.)

(You may read the guidelines through again as they take some time to process this part of the technique. Give them plenty of time to do so and repeat the guidelines to assist them. Pause and read until they indicate that they have completed these instructions. Remember, they can either imagine doing the process or even just pretend to imagine doing the process.)

(When they have completed this part of the technique, thank them and continue to the third part of this technique.)

Take the Data and Information from the experiencing of your New Theories and place them along with the other information of the totalities (add in here also any specific dialogue pertaining to the specific Functions for Totalities they have chosen and are walking through). On the ground, in front of you, between yourself and the third filter. (Give them time to do this or to imagine doing this or to pretend to imagine doing this. You might repeat the instructions to assist them with this process. When you know they have completed this, continue with the technique.)

"Thank you, Now, if you may, please, with all of your life's experiences, filtering to your choosing, continuing, of your, choosing, gather Knowledge, Discernings, Understandings, for your Life's Completeness. Of your choosing, Create or imagine to Create Models, Beliefs, as you choose and for you to use, to share with yourself, with others in your life, for Your Wholeness of Life. Create or imagine or pretend to imagine to Create your Language processes, your Behaviors, the way you Express and Expand you, as a Whole, Entire Being, of your choosing. Process the Data, Information, Dialogues, New Theories, Experiences and Applications and you Choose or imagine or pretend to imagine your Knowledge from all this. You choose or imagine to choose, your Discernments of all this. You may Expand on Similarities and adjust Differences, you may Add to or Delete from, of your choosing, for your processes of Being and Expressing of your Wholeness. Your words, their placement in your Expressions, your Doings, for your Expressions, the Whole Representation of the Totality of you and your life's experience, Choosing the Knowledge gained, choosing the ability to Discern, to Create your Whole life, according to your choosing as you imagine or pretend to imagine it to be, of your choice.. Each aspect from the Data and Structure through the Information and the Patterns, the Knowledge and Discernments with the Processes, all Open to one another, matching Similars with one another, adjusting any Deviations or Anomalies with one another and becoming more One, Whole, Unified, in a common Purpose, Expression, Creating, ongoing throughout your Whole life's Experience and Expressing. All that you may imagine or pretend to imagine, you may Create and be One within yourself, in charge of your life's Experience. Continually Creating New Life's Models, open to the Information and Theories, newly on going and Data and Experiences and Creating Processes and Models for continual New Expressions in a literal sense and new Creations in your life." (Give them time to process this part of the technique you may read this until they have completed the instructions. Add in any other specific instructions pertaining to the specific Function they have placed on the ground.)

(When they have completed this part of the technique, thank them and have them step off the last Function Filter and go to where they began and walk straight through the beginning point to the last Filter, get off again, go to the beginning point and walk to the end again and again until you notice a subconscious shift in them.)

# Chapter 9

# FIELDS OF HUMAN CONSCIOUSNESS

The Human System is made of Mind, Emotion, and Body. The Human system is the whole field made up of the three other fields working together:

Mind (Mental)

Emotion (Spirit)

Body (Physical)

The Reality Principle of a system as a whole field made up of three other fields working together:

Time: Past, Present, Future

Family: Father, Mother, Child

Communication: Transmit, Receive, Message

Reality: Space, Time and Matter

Sin: Guilt, Shame, Fear

Love: Faith, Hope, Charity

Healing: Spiritual, Energy, Physical

All Realities in our universe are made up of tiny atoms. These atoms, though small, take up space. These spaces of atoms and matter are called Dimensions. These Dimensions are:

Dimension: Height/Vertical, Depth/Sagittal, Width/Lateral or Horizonal

There are five levels of human organization:

Individual

Family

Organizational

Society/culture/nation

Global

Nature

Holograms are wholes and whole systems. The universe by nature is Holographic and so are humans and the human body. Human consciousness is holographic as is inner processing and their resulting models, they come naturally.

There are three aspects of Nature: Structure, patterns, and processes.

The world is composed of two different systems the natural systems and the man-made systems.

There is a universal form known as the wholeness model made up of three elemental levels and one totality level. These apply to everything living.

Nature (Totality/Whole System)

Structure (First Element)

Patterns (Second Element)

Processes (Third Element)

Nature will plummet to get us into our patterns and processes. Every system is a whole system, every part of the system has its function within the system to make the system a whole system. Any piece of the system not functioning, no matter the reason, has to be integrated within the whole system for the systems purpose. Otherwise, the system will plummet. Every structure has a purpose. From the structure comes the patterns and processes for the purpose and function. What are our patterns and processes? You'll be thrown out of the center of yourself. This is what happens with cancer. You are throwing yourself away and if you don't get back into the center of yourself you will die. Cancer happens as feed back to be a doormat. You can un-choose to be a door mat. Anger comes because you have standards and don't want them you want other standards. You want to take other standards and plug them into your own.

The Human System (Totality/Whole System)

Mind (First Element)

Emotion (Second Element)

Body (Third Element)

The Human system has three basic functions:

- Identity, basis of Identity and Personality
- Communication /Information Processing and Functions
- Creation

Because human systems are integrated it is possible to observe human information processing as body movement. Movement equals meaning. Nature streamlines systems by having parts or processes at any level that have the same shape or form to resonate together and correspond as one. What part of the airplane flies or the car runs? It is the relationship correspondence, unifying, wholeness that lets the airplane fly, the car operate, and humans function properly.

You are not your senses, your internal organs, your experiences, memories, models, or processes. You are the wholeness combined; the entire system totaled. This is known as Synergy. Synergy is defined as the whole being greater than the sum of its parts.

# Chapter 10

# TOTALITIES OF TRANSFORMATION THEORY

Based on the way we develop Models, Processes, Beliefs (Worldviews). Through Integration, Concepts, Principles, and Models work together.

FACTS:

1. Humans are Natural Systems

2. Humans are Systems

3. The Human System is composed of elements and functions. System Totalities are an entity or aggregation of elements and functions that form a complete whole or totality.

Holographic Learning System & Holographic Health System

The structure of consciousness

Humans have three fields of consciousness; these together made the whole human. Each field of consciousness has two senses in it. Each sense has higher level or abstract, conscious functions for conscious use as a whole.

Mental – Sound & Sight – Identity/Personality

Emotional – Touch & Energy – Communication

Physical – Taste & Smell – Creation

Consciousness of a Personality Field: The sum total of all the movements that represent our Internal Processing's. Our Field of Consciousness is the realm of activity, region of space characterized by a physical property (like gravitational force), where every part of the region has a determinable affect or value. Human Consciousness and Personality, Information and Processing Systems are dimension and have specific location. The Mind Field thinks, reasons, reflects, logic, objective forms hierarchies; is the conscious center of our being. Holograms are Whole Systems (TOTALITY), HUMANS ARE HOLOGRAMS. Human Consciousness is Holographic, Inner Processing is a result of these Models:

Nature:

- Structure
- Pattern
- Process

The World is comprised of two different Systems of Totality:

- Natural Systems
- Man-Made Systems

TIME (Totality):

Past (First Element)

Present (Second Element)

Future (Third Element)

Time itself, is the measure of measurable period during which an action, process or condition exists or continues. Time is non-spatial, and its continuum is measured in terms of the events which succeed one another from the past, through the present, and into the future. One of a series of recurring instances or repeated action added or accumulated quantities or instances. Events, action, processes, or condition can be finite to infinite in duration.

Time is referenced to with various word usage such as:

Nevertheless, Yet (is the same time).

At times (at intervals).

For the time being (for the present).

From time to time (Occasionally).

In no Time: (Very quickly or soon).

In time (sufficiently early).

Time and again (Frequently, repeatedly).

These are all in reference to actions, processes, or condition.

Time itself naturally is designed to cause actions, processes, or conditions of the future to naturally turn to a state of disorder. his is a very natural part of time as actions, processes, or conditions must constantly change for Future movement. There are many aspects showing the way the Earth, Mankind, business, life itself is constantly changing. Time can actually be used itself to be a part of being able to change the continuum of natural disorder of future movements (Time), measurements between actions, processes or conditions. This Natural Disorder is partly due to the unavailable energy in any Closed System and any Systems becomes a Closed System when it is not changing constantly between past, present, and future measurements, which is the meaning and Function of Time. The Unavailable energy in a Closed System will vary directly with any reversible change depending upon the degree of disorder required for the degree of change for Future actions, processes, or conditions within any given system.

# PHYSICS LAWS AND HOLOGRAPHIC HUMAN THEORY

Similarity: Expand.

Unity: Oneness, Identity, Element.

Integrate: Unite, Form, Coordinate into a functioning purpose.

Correspondence: Governs Function. Nature having parts or processes at any level, of the same shape or form resonate as one. Similar parts change together. Example: two electrons when one changes it's spin the other one changes it's spin also. The Totality of related parts that are in a complex whole naturally correspond and affect each other, leaving the Multiplicand unchanged.

The Human System IS A WHOLE SYSTEM so can unify parts that are very different!!!!!!!

Integration: Integrated Systems, Elements, and Function are interrelated and interdependent upon other Elements and Function. Changing one Element of an Integrated System affects the rest of the system entirety. Integration is the process of making Whole and this works due to Correspondence, Unity, Reality, and Wholeness Principles. There are 4 types of Integration Systems or Models: 1) Symbolic, 2) Energetic, 3) Whole Body, 4) Linguistic.

Integrity is the condition of being Whole or complete. To integrate is the process of making Whole. Integrity exists because the structure and processes of Natural Systems are Unified in a way that causes parts to work together in Parallel, Similarities, and Correspondence.

A keyway of attaining greater correspondence and being more Open is to create ways to increase the flow of information throughout the entire system. Communication (Transmit, Receive, Message). As human beings, the information comes into us through our human senses. Human sense is how we experience our lives. From our conscious experience, through our human senses, we create models of our world. These models become our thoughts, feeling, behaviors, our beliefs, values, lifestyles, and circumstances.

The two basic systems of change we can do are Incremental Change & Transformative Change.

Incremental change: Making small shifts in different human behaviors or systems. These incremental changes can be endless.

Incremental change:

- ➢ Success patterns exploring possibilities for patterns or systems for change. Exploring to find patterns for success.
- ➢ Extend and improve the patterns and systems for the change. Repeat the pattern over and over again.
- ➢ The system reached its potential and also shows its built-in problems and is not open to new information, data and feedback.

Transformative change:

- ➢ Success patterns exploring possibilities for patterns or systems for change.
- ➢ Extend and improve the patterns and systems for change. This is usually a process of repetition of the success patterns or systems for change.
- ➢ Success patterns considering anomalies (problems built into the system of success from the start. Taking in new information, data and feedback for change). This is where the original success patterns or systems are taking into anomalies now apparent from the first step of change patterns. Open to feedback, new data, new information, and knowledge. Address anomalies and create new success pattern which addresses the anomalies and go to Step 2 again. Repeat, repeat, repeat, pattern.

## Transformation Theory

Human beings have characteristics and attributes representative of sympathies, frailties, strengths and by nature of their minds can process and evaluate their lives and many other things. They have a conscious existence and may perceive and conceive other things into a real existence. Humans, by their very nature have transformed their actions and processes not only of our world, even DNA and many other living things.

In order to Transform, the key of the formula affecting Transformation is Function. Function is a literal operation that converts one thing into another. The components of changing Function are:

1. Delete
2. Insert
3. Permutation (rearrange)

Genetic modification happens in a bacteria by inserting DNA from another bacteria cell.

Correspondence is the Physics Law governing this process of Function.

Integration is a process of Unifying (Unity).

Humans Transform and Integrate by nature. Their inherent sense of right and wrong, in accordance with and determined by their very nature. Our ability to increase our Function by deleting, inserting, or rearranging things in our lives or environment. Permutation is a major and fundamental change (as in character or condition) based primarily on rearrangement of existent Elements. Changing by act or process, the lineal order of and ordered set or arrangements of character or conditions.

Transformative change is unpredictable about the way the system will be with transformative change. This is change on an identity level.

Transformative change:

1. Success patterns exploring possibilities for patterns or systems for change.
2. Extend and improve the patterns and systems for change. This is usually a process of repetition of the success patterns or systems for change.
3. Success patterns considering anomalies (problems built into the system of success from the start. Taking in new information, data and feedback for change). This is where the original success patterns or systems are taking into anomalies now apparent from the first step of change patterns. Open to feedback new data, new information and knowledge. Address anomalies create new success pattern which addresses the anomalies and go to Step 2 again. Repeat, repeat, repeat, pattern.

Helpless, hopeless, worthless, are key words that the individual is no longer living in their own space, environment, self. There's too much garbage in it to live there. The more we move toward the structure, (space, environment, self) the more effective we are. The more we move away from, deny, refuse and repress, the more abstract we become, the less effective we become. So, to just think or talk about a problem doesn't help. We must deal with the model or structures of the problem and we become more effective.

Humans as individuals are created to self organize, to have unity, correspondence, similarities, within itself. When these do not listen and respond to each other, there is deterioration. This happens on an individual basis as well as in families, communities, countries and the world. Once the system is in decline, it moves quickly to chaos (disorder). Chaos in physics is a form of disorder that is discontinuous and nonlinear but not totally random disorder and degeneration.

Integrity: The condition of being whole or complete. To integrate is the process of making whole. Integrating exists because the structure and processes of natural systems are unified in ways that cause parts to work together in parallel similarity and correspondence. The Natural True Self.

Human Transformation Theory, the way we develop models, paradigms and world views.

Holographic Learning Systems

Holographic Health System

Integrations, concepts, principles and models work together.

Facts:

- Humans are natural
- Humans are systems
- The Human system is composed of parts or elements.

System: An entity or aggregation of elements or parts that form a complete whole or totality. The Three Elements of being human: 1) Mind, 2) Emotions, 3) Body

Universal Law or Principle, Similarity, and Correspondence.

Correspondence: Nature having parts or process at any level, of the same shape or form resonate as one.

Principle of Correspondence: Similar Parts change together. Example: 2 electrons, when 1 changed its spin the other 1 changed also.

Human Systems (Natural Being); 3 Basic Functions:

1. Basis of Identity or Personality
2. Communication and Information Processing Functions
3. Creation

Element of each system of the Natural Being: Mind, Emotion, Body.

Functions of each Element of the Natural Being: Identity, Communication, Creation.

Higher level abstract functions thinking for each of the senses.

Unity: Unifying aspects of naturally integrating systems. The Totality of related parts that is a complex whole.

Unity Principal: Quality or State of being made One, continuity without deviation or change as in Purpose of actions.

Integrating Systems: Elements are interrelated and interdependent. Changing one element of an integrating system effects the rest of the system. Changing one part of a system changes all other parts. The human system is a Whole system so can unify parts that are very different.

Correspondence: Union of similar parts.

Unity: Union of parts that are dissimilar.

Consciousness/Personality Field, the sum total of all the movements that represent our internal processing's. A Field is a realm of activity, region of space characterized by a physical property. (Like, gravitational force, where every point of the region has a determinable affect or value).

Human Consciousness Is A Field. Mind Field thinks, reasons, reflects, logical, objective, forms hierarchies; conscious center of Identity/Personality.

Living Systems are Open Systems. Open Systems take in feedback, data, and energy, from the environment. Modalities are channels to receive the input from the environment. Sub modalities are modalities divided into smaller chunks and more detailed break downs. Sensory Symbolize through the Modalities and or the Sub modalities Energy System or currents of invisible energy flows through the body to revitalize and regenerate cells and body systems. Body Systems can be blocked by such things as anxiety, depression, anger, fears, and cravings.

Seven Senses Modalities of receiving and processing: Sound & Sight, Touch &Energy, Taste & Smell, & Time.

Integration is to make whole; this works due to both Unity and Correspondence Principles and The Reality Principle and The Wholeness Principle.

Reality Principle: We do not know the difference between real or imagined.

Wholeness Principle: The unifying force which holds us together, inner unification comes from the macro-system to live and grow. "What we resist, persists". This force promotes Integration of all our parts, so "What we resist persists".

Data Processing's Sequence:

1. Reception
2. Processing (internally)
3. Storage (as Models and Memories)
4. Transmission (Models and Memories transmitted through language, behaviors, disease)

# Chapter 11

# SENSORY FIRING ORDERS

Reference Modality: Personality firing order.

Personality: A pattern of collective character behaviors, temporal, emotional, and mental traits.

Universal Sequences of firing order from first sense fired. There is a specific pattern the senses fire for each personality profile.

References Senses: $1^{st}$ and $4^{th}$ senses fired.

Decision Senses: $2^{nd}$ and $5^{th}$ senses fired.

Motivator Senses: $3^{rd}$ and $6^{th}$ senses fired.

The First 3 senses fired is External reference and processed. The way we process also the Environment, external (World View).

The Last 3 senses fired are Internal references and processed (Self View). It is the senses we process self.

Personality Profiles and Processing cycles; overall firing patterns:

## IDEALIST FIRING ORDER:

1) Sound: Reference Values and Meaning

2) Touch: Decision Relationships

3) Taste: Motivator Character, Processes

4) Sight: Reference Ideas, Reason, Concepts

5) Smell: Decision Strategies

6) Energy: Motivator Action and Intuition

## CONCEPTUALIST FIRING ORDER:

1) Sight: Reference Ideas, Reason and Concepts

2) Smell: Decision Strategies

3) Energy: Motivator Actions and Intuitions

4) Sound: Reference Values and Meaning

5) Touch: Decision Relationships

6) Taste: Motivator Character

## RELATIONALIST FIRING ORDER:

1) Touch: Reference Touch

2) Taste: Decision Character

3) Sound: Motivator Values and Meaning

4) Energy: Reference Action and Intuition

5) Sight: Decision Ideas, Reasons, Concepts

6) Smell: Motivator Strategies

## ACTIONIST FIRING ORDER:

1) Energy: Reference Actions and Intuition

2) Sight: Decision Ideas, Reason and Concepts

3) Smell: Motivator Strategies

4) Touch: Reference Relationships

5) Taste: Decision Character

6) Sound: Motivator Values and Meaning

## FUNCTIONIST FIRING ORDER:

1) Taste: Reference Character

2) Sound: Decision Values and Meaning

3) Touch: Motivator Relationships

4) Smell: Reference Strategies

5) Energy: Decision Actions and Intuition

6) Sight: Motivator Ideas, Reason and Concept

## STRATEGIST FIRING ORDER:

1) Smell: Reference Strategies

2) Energy: Decision Actions and Intuition

3) Sight: Motivator Ideas, Reason and Concept

4) Taste: Reference Character

5) Sound: Decision Values and Meaning

6) Touch: Motivator Relationships

"Personality overlays" are imprints from the parents and society. These personality overlays and imprints which come through the first three senses fired as based upon the 7 different sensory firing orders. The brain will fire from either the right or left side first and then will cross over to the other side. The first side fired is the world view side. The world view side is where the personality overlays are imprinted from the parents and society. These overlays and imprints include every aspect related to the sense fired to create the view. These aspects are going to include our past, present and future, our values, reasons. Relationships, intuition and actions, our character beliefs and our belief of strategies. All sensory aspects of our world view come from our parents and society.

The World view as compared to the Self view are 2 separate functioning parts of our sensory data and the programs they create.

World view is the way and the areas of interest we notice and are aware of in our world and in our environment. We will not notice nor be aware of things in our environment that are not within the first three senses fired which make up our world view. This view is also going to be made of our personality overlays from our parents and society and our environment. Our World view is not going to be just, fair, and or accurate. Our world view is also a program created in our subconscious by sensory data from our first three senses fired. Having the personality imprints overlaid in these sensory programs creating our world view can cause us problems. perceiving reality in our world around us. By our natural ability, we will see based upon the personality overlay of our parents and society.

The technique (process) of the World View and Self View Questioning helps integrate the 2 different views.

World view is a reflection of Self view. Change Self view and World view will also change. World view serves the purpose of getting Self view to face its Uncertainties, doubts, limiting beliefs, Self-views self-denial, self-refusal and self-repression.

There is nothing in the world that we can see that we are incapable of responding to and dealing with appropriately. If we can see it, we can function healthy and even grow with it.

# REFLECTIVE VIEW TECHNIQUE

World View Self View Questioning Process

Depending upon your firing order place these question suggestions in your firing order. WV=World View. SV=Self View.

Firing Orders: The World view question directly relates to the Self view question. The firing order for each personality profile lays out in the following order for World view and Self view Questioning:

- 1 to 4 (Reference Senses)
- 2 to 5 (Decision Senses)
- 3 to 6 (Motivator Senses)

Idealist

WV 1. Sound: What value or meaning do you seem to notice most often about the environment or the world around you?

SV 4. Sight: Within you is a vision, an idea, you can see, know, things about this, here to help, see it and share it please.

WV 2. Touch: Who feels to you to be the most important relationship in your environment or the world around you?

SV 5. Smell: You have beliefs and step by step strategies to address this situation and even prevent further problems with it, describe these.

WV 3. Taste: Explain the most important character trait in your environment or in the world around you?

SV 6. Energy: You have an intuition, you have an action to be able to offer strength and healing here, speak about this please.

Conceptualist

WV 1. Sight: Regarding things you see most often in the environment explain the reasons you consider these to be so.

SV 4. Sound: What meaning or value do you personally have to offer in this?

WV 2. Smell: In noticing the steps taken by others , in your environment or in the world around you what beliefs appear most significant to you?

SV 5. Touch: You have an ability to relate with this in a beneficial manner, describe this ability.

WV 3. Energy: The actions you most often notice in the environment or the world around, seem to be triggered by what intuitions from others?

SV 6. Taste: Character traits within you are a strength to help you and perhaps others regarding the situation, describe them please.

Relationalist

WV 1. Touch: Who feels to you to be the most important relationship in your environment or in the world around you?

SV 4. Energy: You have an intuition, you have an action to be able to offer strength and healing here, speak about this please.

WV 2. Taste: Explain the most important character trait in your environment or in the world around you?

SV 5. Sight: Within you is a vision, an idea, you can see, know, things about this, here to help, see it and share it please.

WV 3. Sound: What value or meaning so you seem to notice most often about the environment or in the world around you?

SV 6. Smell: You have beliefs and step by step strategies to address this situation and even prevent further problems with it, describe these.

Actionist

WV 1. Energy: The actions you most often notice in the environment or the world around, seem to be triggered by what intuitions from others?

SV 4. Touch: You have an ability to relate with this in a beneficial manner, describe this ability.

WV 2. Sight: Regarding things you see most often in the environment explain the reasons you consider these to be so.

SV 5. Taste: Character traits within you are a strength to help you and perhaps others regarding the situation, describe them please.

WV 3. Smell: In noticing the steps taken by others, in your environment or in the world around you what beliefs appear most significant to you?

SV 6. Sound: What meaning, or value do you personally have to offer in this?

Functionist

WV 1. Taste: Explain the most important character trait in your environment or in the world around you?

SV 4. Smell: You have beliefs and step by step strategies to address this situation and even prevent further problems with it, describe these.

WV 2. Sound: What value or meaning so you seem to notice most often about the environment or in the world around you?

SV 5. Energy: You have an intuition, you have an action to be able to offer strength and healing here, speak about this please.

WV 3. Touch: Who feels too yo to be the most important relationship in your environment or in the world around you?

SV 6. Sight: Within you is a vision, an idea, you can see, know, things about this, here to help, see it and share it please.

Strategist

WV 1. Smell: In noticing the steps taken by others, in your environment or in the world around you what beliefs appear most significant to you?

SV 4. Taste: Character traits within you are a strength to help you and perhaps others regarding the situation, describe them please.

WV 2. Energy: The actions you most often notice in the environment or the world around, seem to be triggered by what intuitions from others?

SV 5. Sound: What meaning, or value do you personally have to offer in this?

WV 3. Sight: Regarding things you see most often in the environment explain the reasons you consider these to be so.

SV 6. Touch: You have an ability to relate with this in a beneficial manner, describe this ability.

Integrate exists because of structure and processes. Natural Systems are unified in ways that cause parts to work together in parallel through the Laws of Similarities and Correspondence. Integrations of Concepts, Principles, and Models all working together. Elements are Interrelating and Interdependent without Deviation or change as in Purpose of Action, Beginning, or Forming Phase. Purpose increases and grows as a natural part of progressing. Challenges and changes are a natural aspect of purpose and is built into our system from the beginning.

Unity in physics is the unifying aspects of Naturally Integrating Systems, with a quality or state of being Multiple. Intent is the determination of the system the Inertia of the System, from the Beginning. Intent being the backbone of purpose, firmly steadfast, fixed and directed. Determined or resolved, having the mind focused, the mental determination of action and result based upon the Intent behind the purpose.

Concept: Something conceived in the mind, thoughts, motion.

Principles: Fundamental law, assumptions, laws or facts of nature and living the working of an artificial device (axiom). Axioms are self-evident truth that requires no proof, universally accepted principles or rules. A proposition assumed without proof for the sake of studying the consequences that follow from it. This is self-evident and obvious. In choice, the axiom of choice is that, given any collection of disjointed sets, a set can be constructed that it contains one element from each of the given sets.

Similarities/Correspondence: Elements with similarities naturally correspond with one another

Concepts/Principles/Models: These naturally work together based upon the physics of Correspondence.

Interrelated/Interdependent without Deviations or change of Purpose of action, acknowledging the individual identity of each aspect within any given system. All-natural law of correspondence, without this interrelating-interdependently, the system becomes more dysfunctional. When these elements and principles are working together based upon the physics of correspondence, the system(s) as a whole function properly and progresses.

Natural disorder is a part of inert uniformity, entropy, and closed systems to get the system to progress and change. Your life's experience is based upon your acknowledging of your true self inner strengths. Your Reality is a reflection of your own Uncertainties, Doubt, and Limiting Beliefs; all you Deny, Refuse, and Repress. Take Time to change the Continuum of Natural Disorder which just occurs to Future. To change by Nature, Function and Condition must be changed. Function consists of progression, and condition involves intent.

In order to Transform, change Function, Function is changed by:

1. Delete

2. Insert

3. Permutation

Integrate (Unity), the sense of right and wrong

$E=mc^2$

E/ Energy; Potential Difference =

m/ Mass

c/ Speed of Light

Ø / Energy spent to respond, Energy to respond dissipates and is not real energy.

The E/ Energy. The potential difference can multiply it's potential difference by 10 times at the mass at the speed of light from the environment. Choose a potential difference of the mc2 and create a state, condition and outcome of the greater difference. Place the state, condition and outcome into the expression to the mass. This can be done, guided imagery, reality principle process, and just thought through based upon elements of Energy of identity.

X/ Times/ X=Position

The Energy within the individual is the potential difference between what is possible/capable in the person and what the mass (environment) is sending at them. As a general response of the natural human, we respond instead of creating a difference, thereby increasing the mass instead of taking charge of the mass. Energy is literally "potential difference", it isn't blind, rampant, or illiterate power. Energy is true power; the exponential of the power. The reason, purpose, potential, and the difference ability within, in regards to literally, the "mass", all around the energy.

We are quantum events in a unified field, impulses of intelligence that have learned how to create all this universe and therefore we as human beings are not self-contained. We are in fact focal points in the unified field. As in the atom, so is the universe. As in the human body, the cosmic body.

# Chapter 12

# QUANTUM LEAPS

Human Beings have characteristics and attributes representative of frailties, sympathies, strengths, and by nature of their minds can process and evaluate their lives and many other things. Perceiving into existence anything that is a part of their dendra. Dendra is created for each "Identity" you have. The creation of the emotion is the most important thing to understand. Identity being the sameness of essential or generic character in different instances, sameness in all that constitutes the objective reality of a thing. All the eye can "see" is what a part of your Identity is already. You cannot see what you do not have the Dendra to see. You cannot "see" what you don't already have a "relationship" about with yourself to "Identify" within, or about yourself. The dendrite is the branching protoplasmic processes that conduct impulses toward the body of a neuron. The Dendra is the chemical combination.

Human beings have a conscious existence and may perceive and conceive other things into real existence. Human, by their very nature have transformed their actions and processes not only our world but even on a DNA level of many other living things. In order to Transform, the key of the formula affecting Transformation is FUNCTION. Function is the literal operation that converts one thing into another. Function is changed by doing any or all of the following: Deleting, Inserting, or Permutation.

Genetic modification happens in a bacteria by inserting of DNA from another bacteria cell. Correspondence is the law governing this process of Function. Integration is a process of unifying (Unity). Humans Transform and Integrate by nature. Their inherent sense of right and wrong, in accordance with and determined by their very nature makes this so.

Permutation is major and fundamental change (as in a character or condition), based primarily on rearrangement of existent elements. Changing by the act or process, the lineal order of and ordered set or arrangements of character or conditions. Such as rearranging priorities differently, based upon character or condition change.

A Quantum Leap is an abrupt Transition (as of an electron, an atom, molecule) from one discrete energy state to another.

Identity and sameness of essential or genetic character in different instances. Sameness in all that constitutes the objective reality of a thing. Objective reality being the conscious creation of the reality. The reality of our world view serves the purpose of awakening our greater knowing of our self. Delete, insert, permutate the reality experiences (perceptions) with the knowing of the greater possibilities based upon your true self character or condition, do the greater right. A quality whose effect is to leave the multiplied unchanged (The number that is to be multiplied by another).

Human beings are born with Quantums; 1 per each human sense:

Sound: Right - Sight: Wrong

Touch: God - Energy: Self

Taste: Life - Smell: Death

These Quantums are God-Given and never leave us here on Earth. No matter how hard we may try to numb or quiet them, they never calm down nor just go away.

We have an inner sense of all of these Quantums, and they constantly remind us of their, and our own purpose. When we accept these and listen to them, we are happy and more positive. When we try to ignore or conquer them, we struggle.

Communication being a process by which information is exchanged between individuals through a common system of symbols, signs or behaviors, an exchange of information.

Just as at the Tower of Babel the Lord said, "If they can communicate this well, anything they can imagine they can do". Communication is the key and Correspondence is the Master of Communication by nature.

You already know right from wrong. Debating, justifying, explanations, denials, refusals, revenges, you already know. You are born with this knowing. Your true identity? You already know.

The Unity principle or Law: A totality of related parts, an entity that is a complex or systematic whole. Unifying aspects of Naturally Integrating Systems. A quality or state of being One, not multiple, One Identity. This aspect of Unity is Continuity, without deviation or change as in Purpose of Actions. Any deviation or change is to be taken back to Purpose and multiplied by Purpose.

The Union of parts that are Dissimilar: Structures and Processing's which Deviate from one another in the same System. Action for Deviating Structure or Process may be taken by an Event, Condition or Process and multiplied into Purpose and/or Totality.

Event: The Fundamental entity of observed physical reality represented by a point designated by 3 coordinates of Place and 1 of Time in the Space-Time Continuum postulated by the Theory of Relativity. Events are Outcomes, something that happens, and the fundamental entity observable with a physical reality. Events are done to achieve an end.

Condition: A state of being, sometimes involving adapting or modifying so as to conform from a previously associated response so the stimulus becomes associated with another. Condition involves circumstances and situations to function.

Process: Process involves something going on and is a key in progress. This can be a natural phenomenon marked by gradual changes that lead toward a particular result. Process is establishing a usual routine set of procedures toward an end. This includes integrating sensory information received so that an action or response is generated.

Wholeness Principle: The unifying force in each of us that holds us together, Inner Unification come from the Macro-System to live and to grow. A natural desire for wholeness, unification, wellness, that comes from each living, intelligent aspect of our being to be whole and healthy and a part with us. This is why what we resist, persists. It is a part of us. A unifying force that promotes integration of all aspects of our being. This unifying force is of nature, based on our fundamental choice to live.

It wants us to live and wants to live as each individual cell and so nature itself promotes integration of all our parts.

Synergy: Synergy is the whole greater than the individual parts, this applies to everything.

The interactions of two or more agents for a whole. Whatever the whole is, there are three aspects that are individual to the whole. Systems working together are Synergetic. Systems are enmities or patterns that interact with each other for a process. The relationship between the parts is the fundamentals of its processes.

The conscious field is formed by a unifying force that is intelligent and aware. An individual's level of personal development can be measured by their ability to perceive the field in self and others and the synergy of the whole based on the correspondence and unity of the individual parts together.

Communication: The act or process of transferring Data.

Healing Model consist of 2 approaches:

1. Physical = Nutrition, Fitness, Hygiene Body Maintenance

2. Spiritual = Body System Matrix, Belief Integration, Addictive Systems (Closed), Energy System.

Examples: There are more you can identify.

NATURE: The inherent character or basic constitution of a person or thing. A creative and controlling force in the universe. An inner force and the sum of such forces in an individual. A kind and class distinguished by fundamental and essential characteristics. The origin of the natural condition.

Structures: The action of building. Arranged in a definite pattern of organization. The arrangement of particles and parts into a substance or body. Organization of the parts as dominated by the general constitution and character of the whole. The aggregate of elements of an entity in their relationship to one another. "Of", relates to or being a method in which each step of the solution to the problem is contained in a separate sub-program.

Pattern: A form or pattern proposed for imitation. A natural or chance configuration. A reliable sample of traits acts tendencies and other observable characteristics. A discernable coherent system based on the intended interrelationship of component parts. Refluent or widespread incidences.

Processes: To progress, advance, ongoing and proceed. Natural phenomenon marked by gradual changes that lead toward a particular result. A continual natural or biological activity or Function. The prominent or projecting part of the structure. To subject to a special process. To subject or handle through an established routine set of procedures

LANGUAGE PROCESSING:

Symbolic: Consisting of proceeding by meaning of symbols, of, relating to or constituting on symbols.

Energetic: Energy and it's transformations, the total energy relation and transformations of a physical, chemical or biological system. To impact energy to, ACT.

Whole Body: Having all its proper parts or components, complete physical being.

HUMAN WHOLENESS:

Mind:

Emotions:

Body:

HUMAN SYSTEM:

Identity, Personality:

Communication, Information Processing (Function):

Creation:

NUMBERS 1 & 2 & 3 ARE ELEMENTS.

LETTERS ARE THIER ASSOCIATED FUNCTIONS.

1): Mind, 1): Mental, 1): Perception Filter

A): Identity and Personality

B): Data, symbols, letters, numbers, music notes, pictures

C): Models, a collection of the memories in Symbols forming internal representations of the memories

D): Structure: arranging in a definite pattern or organization arranged of particles or parts.

E): Forming: Exploring symbols of possibilities until success patterns are discovered or invented, the essential nature of a thing as distinguished from it's matter. (Matrix).

F): Real: Genuine, being what the name implies (precisely) occurring or existing in actuality. Existing as a physical entity and having properties that immovable things having objective independent existence. Belonging to or having Elements or Components that belong to the set of real

G): Space a limited extent in 1, 2 or 3 dimensions, boundless 3 dimensional extent in which objects and events occur and have relative parts and direction, (can be independent of what occupies or occurs in it).

H): Symbolic: Consisting or proceed by means of symbols. Of or relating to or constituting in symbols.

2): Emotions,

A): Communication and Information Processing and storage.

B): Experience and New Theories Filter, Dialoguing the Data into meaningful patterns such as math, physics, information thru Processing Functions, applying the Information into experiences and creating New Theories from the Information and experience into meaningful Patterns.

C): Paradigm: A philosophical or theoretical framework of a scientific or discipline within which theories, laws and experiments in support of the laws are performed.

D): Processes: A natural phenomena marked by gradual changes that lead to a particular result.

E): Norm: Repeating experiences and creating new information and new theories over and over.

F): Vicarious: Experienced or realized through imagination or sympathetic participation in the experience of another.

G): Time: The measurable period during which an action, process or condition exists or continues. A non-spacial continuum that is measured in terms of events which succeed one another through Past, Present to Future. One of a series of recurring or repeated actions, added or accumulated qualities or instances.

H): Energetic: Energy and it's Transformation, the Total energy relation and transformations of a physical, chemical or biological system. To impact energy to ACT.

3): Body, Understanding and Discernment Filters

A): Transmission of Models, memories, thru language and behaviors

B): Knowledge: application and productive use of information and experiences built from experience and New Theories, gaining new understanding and discernments of self and others.

C): Worldview: A comprehensive conception or appreciation of the world from a specific standpoint. (Weltanschauung).

D): Patterns: Natural or chance configuration, a discernable coherent system based on the intended interrelated workings of component parts.

E): Fulfill: Success being achieved, growth now achieved by Integrative differences and modifications into the original Patterns, attain fulfillment of possible expressions.

F): Genetic: Of relating to cause by origin DNA and RNA that determine specific amino acids sequences and appear uniform for nearly all known forms of life.

G): Matter: Substance of physical object is composed material substances occupies space, has mass and is composed predominantly of atoms, consisting of protons, neutrons and electrons, that constitutes the observable universe and is Intervertible with energy.

H): Whole body.

Quantum Leaps and Unbridgeability

Unbridgeability is about choice. Unbridgeability is to be against, to be unaccepted, unabsorbed, unaccredited, and unacknowledged. Choice is a quantum leap syndrome. Quantum leap syndrome is a Matrix continuum of sets of elements placed in a Mathematical continuum.

There are 3 different aspects regarding Choice: 1) Take Action, 2) Take no Action, 3) Let another Take Action. Choice being an option, alternative, preference, selection, and/or election. Be willing to let go to be self and God. Nurture self when others are not willing to choose to go with you, they choose to stay.

Resistance occurs when associated quantums aren't bridgeable. Bridging the quantums incorporates the physics of correspondence. The continuum of opposites and opposition by taking one element of each set and adding it to the other elements of the same or another set.

Bridging the Quantum's take you to a point of Transformation. When bridging the quantums, you bridge from the left side to the right side. Beginning from the top of the Map to the bottom of the Map. Combining Wrong with Right, Self with God, and Death with Life.

Quantum Leaps:

> Right and Wrong

Right: Conforming with or conformable to justice, law. Continue from above. Not spurious, genuine. Just, sound, legal, proper, toward, on the right, in a straight line. Being in accordance with what is just, good, or proper. Conforming to facts or truth.

Wrong: Not on conformity with fact or truth, incorrect or erroneous. In a wrong course, sometimes contrary to. An unjust or injurious act, to go astray or alter. Principles, practices, or conduct contrary to justice, goodness, equity, or law. Not right or proper according to a code, standard or convention.

> God and Self

God: The supreme or ultimate reality; the Being perfect in power, wisdom, and goodness who is worshipped as creator and ruler of the universe. A being or object believed to have more than natural attributes and powers and to require human worship, one controlling a particular aspect or part of reality.

Self: The total, essential, particular being of a person. The entire person of an individual, the realization or embodiment of an abstraction. An individual's typical character or behavior. The union of elements (as body, emotions, thoughts, and sensations) that constitute the individuality and identity of a person. Of the same character throughout, of the same material. Many words beginning with "self" have been added to the dictionary.

> Life and Death

Life: The property or quality that distinguishes living. To continue from above. A principle or force that is considered to underlie the distinctive quality of animate beings. The sequence of physical e process of living. A specific phase of earthly existence. The form or pattern of something existing in reality.

Death: The act of dying, termination of life. A permanent cessation of all vital functions. The cause or occasion of loss of life.

These synthesis with:

Sound; Right

Sight; Wrong

Touch; God

Energy; Self

Smell; Death

Taste; Life

The Quantum Leaps are a Continuum. A continuum is a coherent whole characterized as a collection, sequence, or progression of values or Elements varying by minute degrees. Good and bad stand at opposite ends of a continuum instead of describing the two halves of a line (Wayne Shumaker). The set of real numbers include both the rationales and the irrationals: broadly; a compact set which cannot be separated into two sets neither of which contains a limit point of the other. It is continuous.

There must needs be opposition in all things and the Quantum Leaps are opposites; Right/Wrong, God/Self, Life/Death. Each of the Abstract or Conscious Functions apply to each Quantum relating to its position on the Holographic Human Map as well as the sense it is with. There can be no Right without Wrong nor Wrong without Right. There can be no God without Self nor Self with God. There is no Life without Death or Death without Life. I have heard it said that in a "Sense", there is no Right or Wrong, there is no God or Self, there is no life or Death. Pick and choose for yourself, but don't let the interpretations of man lead you astray. It is also stated in scriptures that Lucifer will tell you 99 truths to get you to believe 1 lie.

Infinity Technique (Experiential Quantum Leap Questioning Process)

There is always a Transition or Crossover point. We have mentioned prior of a 7th Sense, a sense of Self and/or a sense of Time. This 7th sense has the Primary Question "When?". As with the other quantum's, this sense also represents the other Abstract, Conscious, and Subconscious Functions already a part of this on the Holographic Human Map. This 7ths sense, as relating to the Quantum Leap represents the Great, I Am and the Eternal Now. This is the Transition Point the quantum's take to Leap, the Crossover point from one side of the Map to the opposite side.

# PHYSICS OF CORRESPONDENCE: WHOLENESS

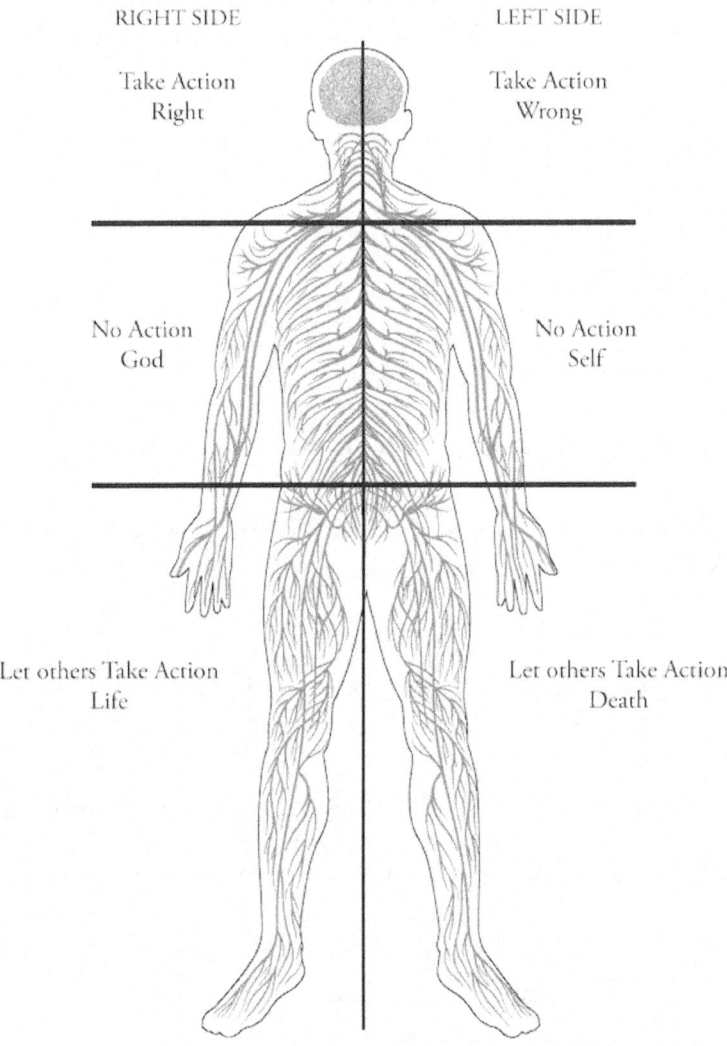

The Quantum Leap begins in the center, at the Great I Am and Eternal Now, goes from there to the upper left of the map (Wrong), down to Self, then to Death. This process completes the left side of the Body Map and the Quantum's continue at the Transition or Crossover Point. The Center of the Map, the Great I Am, Eternal Now, from here the Quantum

Leap continues to the upper right side of the Holographic Human Map, (Right), continuing down from here to the right center, "God", and then down to "Life". From Life the Quantum Leaps continues to the center, the Transition Point, the Crossover, "When"? the Great I Am, the Eternal Now.

Begin Technique:

Transformative Change

Identity Level Change

Quantum Bridging is about Choice, Change, Goals, and Being

Be Willing to let go – To Be One with Self and God

WHEN (stand on). When is at the Center, the great I AM and Eternal NOW. The center is where the Quantum Leap begins. When are you ready to begin?

WRONG (stand on). Sensory symbolize this Quantum with a Shape and a Color.

SELF (stand on). Sensory Symbolize this Quantum with an Energy.

DEATH (stand on). Sensory symbolize this Quantum with a Smell.

While focusing on these three sensory<br>symbols, please walk to the Center.

WHEN (stand on). When is at the crossover point. The Center. Quantum Leaps transition at the crossover point. When are you ready to use your function, and make this leap?

RIGHT (stand on). Sensory symbolize this Quantum with a Sound.

GOD (stand on). Sensory symbolize this Quantum with a Texture or Temperature.

LIFE (stand on). Sensory symbolize this Quantum with a Taste.

> While focusing on these three sensory
> symbols, please walk to the Center.

WHEN (stand on). This is the center. Quantum Leaps continue at the center. When are you ready to continue?

WRONG (stand on). Why have you chosen this as a Goal?

SELF (stand on). Which actions can you take to begin or perpetuate this Goal?

DEATH (stand on). Where could your strategies take you regarding this Goal?

WHEN (stand on). When is it time for you to Transition?

RIGHT (stand on). What is the Value and Meaning of this Goal?

GOD (stand on). Who is this goal about?

LIFE (stand on). How do your beliefs about character lead you to success in regard to this Goal?

WHEN (stand on). When is it time to continue?

WRONG (stand on). Why is this Quantum associated with this Goal?

SELF (stand on). With the Energy you feel with this Quantum, Which connections can you make?

DEATH (stand on). Right now, by choice, Where would you choose this Quantum to take you?

WHEN (stand on). When?

RIGHT (stand on). You find extraordinary Value in this goal moving forward, What is the associated meaning to this Quantum?

GOD (stand on). Who is this Quantum in relation to?

LIFE (stand on). How do you believe in your Character of your-self, in regard to this Quantum?

WHEN (stand on). When do you continue this process?

> Quantum Leaps begin at the center, transition at the center, and continue at the center. Please continue to walk this path, focusing on the associated sensory symbols. Your path marks Infinity as it continues by your choosing. When you feel a shift in Self, please continue through Life, to When, and walk forward.

# Chapter 13

## MEMORY-CORRESPONDENCE

MEMORY:

Real: Relating to everyday concerns and activities. Seriously, Genuine.

Vicarious: Even that have been deleted. Imaginative or subjective response in experiences of another. Occurring, unexpected or abnormal. Another's experience of it.

Genetic: Relating to and determined by the origin. Present at birth or development in childhood without needing any instruction. Ancestral, inherited, instinctual or natural.

CLOSED SYSTEM:

Deny:
Refuse:
Repress:

OPEN SYSTEM:

Admit:
Accept:
Express:

SUCCESS:

Form: Explore possibilities until success patterns are discovered or invented

Norm: The success patterns are repeated over and over

Fulfill: Success begins to flatten a bit still rising, growth is now achieved by integrating differences and modifications into the original pattern at this the system reaches it's peak then begins to decline, having attained its fullest possibilities of expression.

WISDOM: The discerning use of knowledge, which body of knowledge is best to use where, when. Being wise means you have an elevated understanding of the entire system.

Data: Symbols themselves, letters, numbers, sensory symbols such as sounds, textures, temperature, sweet, bitter,

Information: Arrangement of data into meaningful patterns (such as math, physics)

Knowledge: Application and productive use of information. Knowledge is built on the models we form out of experience and theories.

DATA PROCESSING:

Reception
Storage
Transmit

META PROGRAMS:
Data Processing
Information Patterns and Storage
Compressing for Model Making

EDUCATE: Unique Qualities, Talents of Each.

A sense of commonality between the individual and their environment, the common thread they have with each other and a bond with the natural world.

A belonging and harmonizing of unique individuality with a sense of commonality.

To Draw Out.

WORLDVIEW:

Individual
Family
Society

SELF VIEW:

Me
Myself
I

SIN:

Guilt
Shame
Fear

PURE LOVE OF CHRIST:

Hope
Faith
Charity

REALITY: The quality or state of being real, the totality of real things and events.

Space: A period of time, and it's duration a limited extent in 1, 2 or 3 dimensions. A boundless 3-dimensional extent in which objects and events occur and have relative position and direction, beyond earth's atmosphere and solar system.

Time: A measurable period during which an action process or condition exists or continues. Non-spatial continuum that is measured in terms of events which exceed one another from past through present to future.

Matter: The substance of which a physical object is composed. Material substance that occupies space, has mass, and is composed predominantly of atoms consisting or protons, neutrons, and electrons, that constitutes the observable universe, and that is interconvertible with energy. A material substance of a particular kind or for a particular purpose.

TIME:

Past
Present
Future

FAMILY:

Father
Mother
Child

COMMUNICATION:

Transmit
Receive
Message

MESSAGE:
Intent
Content
Context

Consciousness is a shape given form by space and dimension.

DIMENSION:

Height
Lateral
Depth

INTEGRATION:

    a   Concepts
    b   Principles
    c   Models

INTEGRITY: Structures and Processes unite to work in Parallels based upon Similarities.

NATURE:

    1)   Structures
    2)   Patterns
    3)   Processes

First Position Upper (Mental) DIRECTION

Elements:

    d   Structure
    e   Data
    f   Forming
    g   Admit
    h   Perceive
    i   Intent
    j   Transmit
    k   Delete

Principles of Correspondence:

a. "Integration" of Unity
   b. "Concepts (with Principles, Models)
   c. "Integrity" "Structure", unified with interrelated "Elements"

"Structure" "Processes" unite "Similar Time, A measurable period during which an action process or condition exists or continues. Non-spatial continuum that is measured in terms of events which exceed one another from past through present to future.

   a. Similiar's". "Process" of Characteristics add or insert.
   b. "Unifying" of "Deviating" "Structure" (event, condition or process)

Second Position Middle (Emotional) QUESTIONING

Integrate, Integrity, Patterns to Interrelated "Elements". Relationships of "Elements" to its Content.

"Principles" already "Interrelated" and "Interdependent"

Elements:

   a. Patterns
   b. Information
   c. Norming
   d. Accept
   e. Receive
   f. Context
   g. Insert

Third Position Lower Physical MODELING

Assign 1 Element of 1 Set to an Element of another set (Contents)

Permutate Character, Condition, rearrange Existing "Elements"

Integrate Process of "related Elements", Similar

"Deviating" processes to Structure "Unity"

Elements:

    a. Processes
    b. Knowledge
    c. Fulfill
    d. Express
    e. Transmit
    f. Content
    g. Message
    h. Permutation

INTEGRATE IS EMOTIONAL AND MENTAL DIMENSIONAL MAP

Interdependent and Interrelated; is Physical Processes

SIMILARS; STRUCTURES TO PROCESSES

DEVIATING; STRUCTURES TO PROCESSES

INTEGRATION:

        i. CONCEPTS
       ii. PRINCIPLES
      iii. MODELS

INTEGRITY:

    A. STRUCTURES
    B. PATTERNS
    C. PROCESSES

## Chapter 14

# INNER UNIFICATION

Correspondence happens in the between anything. The Spirit resides in the between. Correspondence happens through the Spirit. The Spirit is the Substance of Correspondence.

Wholeness is the Unifying Force which holds us together. Inner Unification comes from the Macro-System to live and to grow this is the background for the saying, "What we resist, persists." This natural force for Wholeness promotes Integration of All parts of us and all Whole Systems. The Wholeness Model is made of 3 separate systems and 1 Totality Level. Holograms are elements of the Totality level. Each element has its associated sense and its individual function. Each element corresponds with the other elements based upon the 3 elements which make the whole of correspondence. The Totality is the state of being complete, entirety, Wholeness.

Matrix; 1): Add, 2): Deviations with respect to Time, 3): Multiplication with a Multiplicand. Do this from the left to right. Finding the common denominator as it pertains to Action, Function, Processes. Element; 1, 2, and 3 of each totality. Function of each element within the system, inter-relating, inter-dependently.

Incremental Change: This refers to small shifts in Programs, Models, or Beliefs. Incremental change is endless change and is constantly going through the Disorder process.

Transformation Change: This is unpredictable change and exponential change. This represents an Identity Level change.

Integrity: The condition of being whole or complete. To integrate is the process of making whole. Integrating exists because the structure and processes of natural systems are unified in ways that cause parts to work together in parallel similarity and correspondence. The Natural True Self.

Human Transformation Theory: The way we develop models, paradigms, and world views.

Element of each system of the Natural Being: Mind, Emotion, Body

Functions of each Element of the Natural Being: Identity, Communication, Creation.

Wholeness principle, Oneness, Totality. Each Totality consists of 3 separate elements corresponding together as one, inter-relating, inter-dependently. First element of each totality being Mind and Identity, therefore senses of sound and sight. Second element being Emotion and Communication therefore, touch and energy. Third element being body and creation therefore smell and taste. Add into these the other aspects of the functions of the holographic human and they all fit together, as one whole system well defined and diagrammed out.

Higher level abstract functions, thinking for each of the senses.

Unity, unifying aspects of naturally integrating systems. Unifying aspects of naturally Integrated Systems. The Totality of related parts that is a complex whole.

Unity Principal: Quality or State of being made One, continuity without deviation or change as in Purpose of actions.

Integrating Systems: Elements are interrelated and interdependent. Changing 1 element of an integrating system affects the rest of the system.

Changing 1 part of a system changes all other. The human system is a Whole system so can unify parts that are very different.

Correspondence: union of similar parts.

Unity: Union of parts that are dissimilar. Integrate dissimilar parts for union. Maintaining focus on beginning purpose and intent.

Consciousness/Personality Field: The sum total of all the movements that represent our internal processing's.

Field: A realm of activity, region of space characterized by a physical property. (Like, gravitational force, where every point of the region has a determinable affect or value.)

Human Consciousness Is A Field

Mind Field; thinks, reasons, reflects, logical, objective, forms hierarchies, conscious center of Identity/Personality.

Disorder specifically pertains to the Function of the System as a Whole and so the unavailable energy is a natural, normal Function of and within the original System, though it has never been recognized in the System, as a Whole and trained of the Systems Function and the role it may play within the System's Function. This is in direct relationship to the things within the System which are mixed up and disorderly since the System's beginning within those involved in its beginning.

Uncertainty within the System specifically refers to the System's own areas of Doubt, skepticisms, suspicion, mistrust, the System's lack of sureness about someone or something. Uncertainty may range from a falling short of certainty to an almost complete lack of conviction or knowledge about an outcome or result. Doubt refers to areas of both uncertainty and inability to make a decision. Skepticism implies unwillingness to believe without conclusive evidence and suspicion stresses a lack of faith in the truth, reality, fairness, or reliability of something or someone. Mistrust implies a genuine Doubt based upon Suspicions.

Uncertainty: The systems lack of sureness about someone or something.

Doubt: The systems inability to make a decision.

Skepticism: Unwillingness to believe without conclusive evidence.

Suspicion a lack of faith in truth, reality, fairness, or reliability of something or someone.

Mistrust: Genuine doubt based upon suspicions.

Disorder within a System might be harder to Deny, Refuse or Repress, while Doubts, Skepticism or Mistrust is easily denied and Closed about.

Causality is the relation between a cause and its effect or between regularly correlated events or phenomena. The reason for an action or a condition or a motive. Motive brings out an effect or a result. A person or thing that was the occasion of action or state. Effect is the antonym of cause. Cause as a verb as to bring to pass to happen the antonym being to destroy. Effect is intent, basic meaning, essence. Something inevitably follows an antecedent as in cause or agent. Appearance, accomplishment, fulfillment. The content of the computer is less important than its effect. Impression. Quality or state of being operational. Cause to come into being, bringing about often by surmounting obstacles. Effect goes beyond mere influence. It refers to actual achievement of a final result. The antonym for effect is cause. Causality; the fact of Being, casually determined, the antonym being spontaneity.

Inert refers to a lacking of the power to move. Deficient in active properties, lacking the usual or anticipated action (naturally already a part of the system's created ability). Inactive; The opposite of inert is vigorous.

Uniformity is a quality or state of being uniform, being of the same form with the rest of the System. Uniform(ity), consistent in conduct or action with interpretation of laws, of the same form within the System, conforming to the rule and mode of the System. Uniformity is relating to or being convergent of a series whose terms are functions in such a manner that the absolute value of the difference between the sum of the first (En) terms of the series and the sum of all terms can be made arbitrarily small for all values of the domain of the functions by choosing the (En-th) sufficiently far along in the series. This process brings the Anomalies into Uniformity.

All this is really about is our ability to grow, succeed, progress, and learn. There is a natural process of growth and change interrelating with one another for survival of the whole. Living systems have great potential. Few living beings, if any, have lived to complete all they were able to. Life gives us challenges, not to destroy nor tear us down, but for our potential and our growth. If you have a challenge, you have the strength to overcome it. If you have a question, you have the answer within already. It is a part of being a natural human and because of the Entropy Cycle that we are pushed to near destruction before we find the INNER strength to overcome. We were never intended to come into this existence just for the purpose of hurt, suffering, pain, failure.

Each separate phase or stage, each separate aspect of any given system, whether natural or man-made has its own specific purpose and Function (Identity), pre-disposed within its Purpose/Function, is the time within the System, that it is to release its Energy to fulfill its purpose within the system's operations. Everything, by Nature, has a Structure, Pattern and Process it is operated by. When these structures, patterns and processes are not followed correctly, or not allowed to Function within their nature, the whole system can come crashing in on itself. Time is a very important aspect of the unavailable, unskilled Energy in any given system. Just as in any success, timing may be crucial to success.

Potential Difference within any given System

Disorder and Uncertainty being referred to as Discontinuous Disorder and Discontinuous Uncertainty, still implies the Disorder and the Uncertainty, just in a sense where the system recognizes the Disorder and Uncertainty, and trains it.

The difference in Potential between two parts that represent the work involved, or Energy released in the transfer of a unit quantity from one point to the other. Potential Energy is the Energy that a piece of matter has because of its position or nature, or because of the arrangement of its parts. It has zero other Potential. It is this very Energy within the system which is causing the Disorder and Uncertainty within the System. It is not "outside forces", nothing outside of the system is the cause of the Disorder and Uncertainty.

Anomalies are indicators of an Entropy cycle. An Entropy is considered a measure of the unavailable Energy in a Closed System that is also usually considered to be the measure of the system's Disorder. This is the property of the system's state that varies directly with any reversible change within the system, to the degree of Disorder or Uncertainty of a system.

Without the opportunity for the Disorder and Uncertainty, the System is held to maintain its status quo. To maintain stability, to be consistent, is indicative of not changing. Were our future to be stable, to have no opportunity for change, our lives would be very different today.

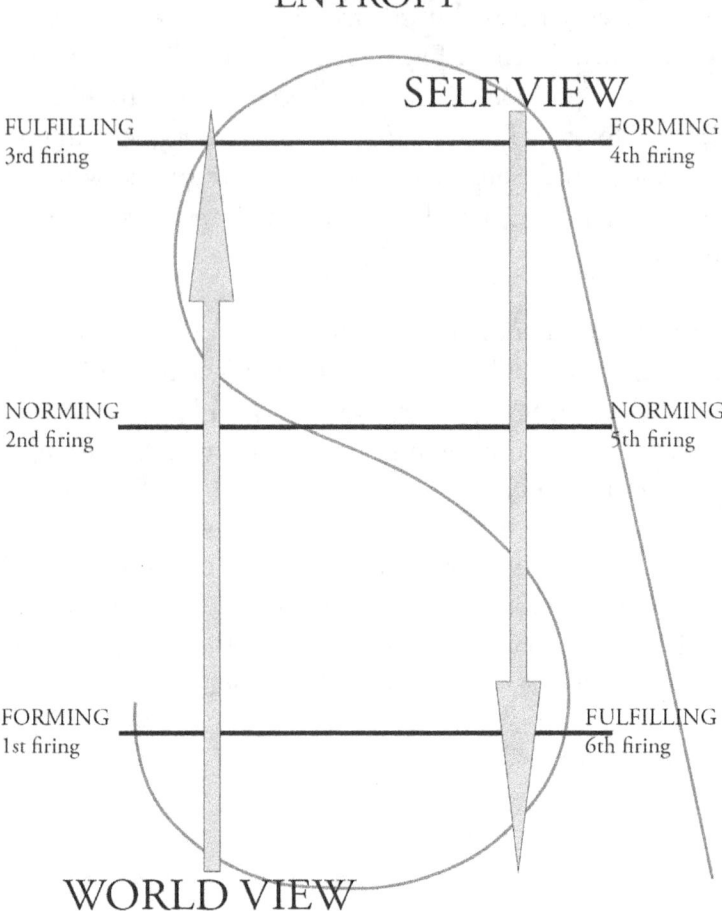

The term itself of "Discontinuous Disorder" and "Discontinuous Uncertainty", are not terms we are familiar with. Discontinuous clearly and simply just means lacking sequence or coherence and the antonym for Discontinuous is obviously "continuous". So, were our lives to be "continuous", they would be continuing sequentially with coherency, in other words, our lives would not change. Our Future would be no different than our past nor would our present. With the Potential ability to change our Future, we get Direction from our Past, we must Question our Present, and we find new Models and Patterns for our Future. The Future is intended, of itself, to be Modeled for Disorder and Uncertainty not for Stability, sequence and coherence. This concept is somewhat new to some of us.

So much of these Holographic Human Theory Models are in some contrast to some of man's teachings. I have also researched scriptures, not only to I not find anything to counter higher level thinking models, I find many scriptures which do counter much of man-made thinking concepts.

The Function of the entropy is to the ultimate state of inert uniformity, a lacking of the power to move. A deficient in active properties due to the lacking of usual or anticipated actions. Simple

put, the entropy (*unavailable Energy) is unskilled. The entropy released its available Energy in an effort to avoid change due to being unskilled to change itself. This is a result of a Closed System, not Open to change to a point of denying, refusing, and repressing any new data. Time itself naturally is designed to cause actions, processes, or conditions of the Future to naturally turn to a state of Disorder. This is a very natural part of time as actions, processes, or conditions must constantly change for Future movement. There are many aspects showing the way of the Earth, Mankind, business, life itself is constantly changing.

Time can actually be used itself to be a part of being able to change the continuum of Natural Disorder of Future Movements (Time), measurements between actions, processes or conditions. This Natural Disorder is partly due to the unavailable Energy in any Closed System and any Systems become a Closed System when it is not changing constantly between past, present, and future measurements. Which is the meaning and Function of Time.

The Unavailable Energy in a Closed System will vary directly with any reversible change depending upon the degree of disorder required for the degree of change for Future actions, processes or conditions, within any given system.

In order to manage these Entropy Cycles in our lives and be able to have Discontinuous Disorder and Uncertainty, we can follow the Matrix Model and Transformation Nature.

When Anomalies come about in your life, that are Similar Anomalies (they seem to (try) take you away from your goal; for they are "out of the box" so to speak, they could happen to anyone). They are Deviating Anomalies when they are more along the lines of disastrous and aren't common. Identify the Multiplicand; the original Function and purpose of the System from its origin using the Deviating Anomalies as the Exponent to times the Function and purpose by.

Example: You begin to go to college to get a degree and problems begin to arise, seemingly attempting to keep you from doing your college. A Similar Anomaly might be realizing you need glasses to read your college books. This could be classified as something common or similar to deal with, in life. A Deviating Anomaly might be more along the lines of losing a scholarship for school, getting expelled from school, losing a loved one, or getting in a horrible accident.

Entropy Cycles: A Statistical Disorder of Energy. The Entropy cycle is a measure of the unavailable Energy in a Closed System that is also usually considered to be a measure of the Systems Disorder. It is a property of the Systems state and will vary in direct regards to any Reversible change in the System and in regard to the Time factors of the Disorder of the Systems Energy which is Unavailable and causing the Disorder. The Degradation of the matter and Energy in the universe, to the ultimate state of Inert Uniformity. The process of Degradation, running down, or the Natural trend to the Disorder.

Anomalies: Information that runs counter to the normal beliefs of the System. They are the defects already a part of the System from the beginning, and they stop the System from growth, just based upon the Natural Order of Time and Future and Disorder.

Entropy

Time

Space

Matter

Natural Disorder

Negentropy

Discontinuous Disorder

Unpredictable Identity

Change and growth takes both Space and Time to come to fruition. The proper, or right location is important. Still, change or growth can only happen in its proper, or right time. As human beings, we can decide (usually) both Space and Time. We have choice on a conscious level. Choice is not always considered for us or others, and Space and Time does not have their own choice. We came to earth to learn, to use our choice (free agency) righteously. Sometimes, Space ends up being decided for us by government agencies or loved ones who have to step in for our, and others safety. Time is entirely up to us in our degree of preparedness for the choice to Change.

Wholeness is The Unifying Force which holds us together. Inner Unification comes from the Macro-System to live and to grow. This is the background for the saying, "What we resist, persists." This natural force for Wholeness promotes Integration of All parts of us and all Whole Systems. The Wholeness Model is made of 3 separate systems and 1 Totality Level. This is a Hologram of each part of the whole of the System.

Totality; The state of being complete, entirety, Wholeness.

TOTALITY; WHOLENESS

1) Similarities: Adding to the Similar Anomalies for Wholeness in present Time.

2) Deviations/Unity: Stop and Question your Whole structure and purpose because the Deviating Anomalies pertain to Time's Elements: 1) Past, 2) Present 3) Future: regarding your Beginning and Purpose of the Totality.

3) Integration/Remembering and focus on the Multiplicand: The original purpose you began this goal or journey for. Scale out the degree of the Deviating Anomaly and Times the Multiplicand by the number of times the Deviating continues.

Matrix:

1) Add: Add similar anomalies into ongoing plan.

2) Deviations: Deviations with respect to Time.

3) Multiplication: Multiplication with a Multiplicand.

OPEN SYSTEM: An Open System has permeable boundaries and is not threatened nor fearful of new experiences in its environment. The Open System is Wise and open to change and progression. The Open System does not necessarily approve of everything in the environment though the Open System seeks to learn whatever it may from all in its surroundings. Open Systems are non-judging but seek only to gain greater knowledge and share their knowing's. Living Systems are Open Systems. Open Systems take in Feedback, Data, and Energy from its environment. Open Systems have different Modalities to receive the input from the environment, simply due to the fact that all its possible areas of the input are Open and not Closed to the input. Take a nail and try to hammer it into cement. It takes a special nail gun to get the cement to allow the nail to penetrate it. Take a nail and try to hammer it into a piece of wood. Not only does the nail go into the wood, but the wood changes also some of its shape inside and out to allow the nail to penetrate it. Things of nature must be Open Systems, or they will die. A tree, a plant, even the seed, and root must be open. If any of these have boundaries which are not permeable and flexible, the tree or plant will die. If the seed or root is closed the plant or tree cannot even grow. This process is continuous in all aspects of our life and it cycles through these three Patterns to maintain an Open System. Open Systems process the Disorder from its environment and the Disorder is naturally Discontinuous Disorder because the system constantly grows.

Admit: This is the first Element of an Open System and is associated with the senses of Sound and Sight. This merely means to allow and permit entrance or access and is specifically referring to what we Hear and See. Simply acknowledging, actually really hearing and really seeing what is said and available to be seen. Simply Admit that it is what was said and seen, no changing, no rejecting, just admitting it was what you did hear and see. Admit; Open Systems Believe the Data coming into the system to the point of Acknowledging the Data. They do not consider it delusional, unreal nor surreal. It Admits and Affirms the Data as having a purpose. It allows the Data to go through the Open Systems for processing anything of importance. Open Systems "Own" the Data coming into it. This means it Believes, Affirms, Admits, and Acknowledges it. Admitted merely means the acknowledgment, perception, actually seeing and hearing what the addict says, how the addict feels and what the addict does. The opposite of admitting is denying and denying would mean saying "no, they did not say and do that, I never saw nor heard them." In very simple terms, this is a first step in admitting verses denying. Again, Admit; Open Systems Believe the Data coming into the system to the point of Acknowledging the Data. They do not consider it delusional, unreal, nor surreal. It Admits and Affirms the Data as having a purpose. It allows the Data to go through the Open Systems for processing anything of importance. Open Systems "Own" the Data coming into it. This means it Believes, Affirms, Admits, and Acknowledges it.

Accept: This is the second Element of an Open System and is associated with the senses of Touch and Energy. Accepting indicates a receiving willingly what has been Admitted without protesting or rejecting any of it. Accept implies having a favorable response, expressing a recognition of something favorably being offered for your benefit or the benefit of the whole. Associated with the senses of Touch and Energy indicates acceptance. Accepting the Data includes the processing of the Data in the Open System. The processing is done without a judgment or reaction. Permitting acceptance of all the Data to be processed, dialogued and New Theories looked at without Protest or Reaction. Accepting the Data includes the processing of the Data in the Open System. The processing is done without a judgment or reaction. Permitting acceptance of all the Data to be processed, dialogued and New Theories looked at without Protest or Reaction. Open Systems having acquired and experienced this new Data. Accepting the Data includes the processing of the Data in the Open System. The processing is done without a judgment or reaction. Permitting acceptance of all the Data to be processed, dialogued and New Theories looked at without Protest or Reaction. Open Systems having acquired and experienced this new Data.

Express: This is the third Element of an Open System and is associated with the senses of Taste and Smell. Expressing is about explicitly displaying your own Character Traits and your own Strategies of accomplishing things with your behaviors. The purpose of your achievements reflecting your personal, specific beliefs. What you do makes clearly known the whole of your inner being. Manifesting your personal beliefs in all of your expressions. A Totality of your words, gestures, actions by your natural impulse being your inner compulsions. Open Systems having acquired and experienced this new Data. Express their new Learning's vigorously and emotionally through their Actions and Communications. Open Systems give voice to their New Awareness. Socially and Intellectually due to the Anomalies and Feedback that is all a part of our Living Cycle, our Being. This allows any data from the environment to be used to improve the system. No environmental feedback can throw an open system into decline when it maintains itself open. An Open System does not feel a need to try to control the feedback, it is not intimidated or anxious or depressed due to the data and feedback. Open Systems having acquired and experienced this new Data. Express their new Learning's vigorously and emotionally through their Actions and Communications. Open Systems give voice to their New Awareness. Socially and Intellectually due to the Anomalies and Feedback that is all a part of our Living Cycle, our Being. This allows any data from the environment to be used to improve the system. No environmental feedback can throw an open system into decline when it maintains itself open. An Open System does not feel a need to try to control the feedback, it is not intimidated or anxious or depressed due to the data and feedback.

CLOSED SYSTEM: It takes a lot of effort to maintain the system as a Closed System. Most any and all Data and Feedback from the environment (outside of the system) must be Denied, Refused and Repressed to keep the system closed. Over a period of time all the efforts involved to be able to Deny, Refuse and Repress any Data or Feedback consumes and controls all thoughts, feelings and behaviors of the Whole of the System until there seems to be no Whole (no Self) left within the system at all. The system literally becomes nothing more than the Personality, Identity, Internal communications, Emotions and Beliefs, Character traits and Strategies just to support the Denial, the Refusal and the Repressing of the Data and Feedback. A Closed System is very predictable. A Closed System is not going to change on its own, it may change with the natural forces of life, but a Closed System is not choosing to change. Closed Systems will also often times deny that they are closed. The more the system is closed, the greater the forces come to attempt to open the system. When you already know the way a person or other system is going to respond to you, that system is predictable, therefore, the system is closed. Closed Systems are not open to new feedback, data or information, let alone knowledge. When a Closed System is in decline, Natural forces come into play, their only goal is to eliminate or lift the restrictions that keep the System Closed. These natural forces can feel like battering rams pounding on the boundaries and walls of the Closed System. This, at times can appear as "tough love", forcing the Whole System towards "hitting rock bottom". Anomalies are indicators of an Entropy cycle. Entropy is considered a measure of the unavailable energy in a Closed System that is also usually considered to be the measure of the systems disorder. This is the property of the systems state and will vary directly with any reversible change within the system, to the degree of disorder or uncertainty of a system. The function of the entropy is to the ultimate state of inert uniformity; a lacking of the power to move. A deficient in active properties due to lack of usual or anticipated actions. Simply put, the entropy (*unavailable energy) is unskilled. The entropy releases its available energy in an effort to avoid change due to being unskilled to change itself.

Deny: Denial: Refuse to admit or acknowledge the truth, negation of logic, a psychological defense mechanism in which problems or reality, oftentimes even refusing to look at the Data or Information. Ascertaining that an allegation is false becomes a negation in logic. Denial becomes a Psychological defense mechanism in which confrontation with a personal problem or with Reality is avoided by denying the existence of the problem or reality. The Opposite of Deny is Admit. Deny is to declare as untrue, refuse to admit or acknowledge or giving a negative answer or response. Denying admittance, at times to a point of something even existing, such as the truth or any valid Data. Contradicting, contravening as true or valid, regardless of what another says or does.

Refusal: The turning down of a proposal. Rejection, disapproval, refusing to accept internal promptings, let alone outside feedback. The act of refusing, rejecting, disapproving and just giving up. The opposite of Refuse is Acceptance. Refusal is an unwillingness to accept, comply, or even answer (respond). Avoiding, in any way possible, justifying, blaming, countering, to consider worthless. Refusing is also rejecting. This is specifically pertaining to the way of acting or relating with ourselves and others.

Repression: Countermeasure, against, revolt. Clamp down, suppression, pacification. The action or processes of repressing: the state of being repressed. A mental process by which distressing thoughts, memories or impulses that may give rise to anxiety and are excluded from consciousness and left to operate in the subconscious. Put down or prevent Natural development. Repressing is responding as if under pressure or injustice. Repress is excluding even from consciousness. Holding back any response to the environment and input. This pertains to the senses of Taste and Smell so Repress applies to the lack of response and such to belief of character, processes and strategies. Adapting behaviors that serve or appear to serve as important functions in achieving success. Closed to the point of creating a Structure or road map to remain closed, filled with tactics, plans operations and research to back it.

Disorder, which is directly related to or based upon and employing the principles related to the System's natural ability to grow and change. Any system must continue to grow. Even when success is achieved, the system has fulfilled its purpose and purpose must continue so growth is inevitable. Growth, by definition, is continual.

Anomalies are events, conditions, processes, that vary from the norm or original plan or Forming Phase of all things man made or natural. These anomalies are unavailable energy, unskilled, originating from the Beginning or Forming Phase. Information that runs counter to the norm, beliefs of the system. They are defects already a part of the system from the beginning that are stopping the system from growing. Anomalies come to make missing parts of the Whole System return.

The degree of severity of the Anomaly are indicative of the degree of disorder or uncertainty of the system from the beginning which is capable of reversible change. Therefore, Anomalies do not come without the possible and potential of change in the system.

The purpose or intent of Anomalies themselves is to make the missing parts of the system whole again. Every functioning system is a whole system and must change and grow to remain a whole system. When Anomalies appear, growth is again achieved by Integrating differences and Modifications into the original pattern or Forming Phase.

Wholeness is the principle intent Anomalies naturally work to achieve.

Wholeness Principle: The Unifying Force which holds us together, inner unification comes from the macro-system to live and grow. What we resist, persists. This force promotes Integration of all parts. Integrate, exists because of structure, and processes. Natural Systems are unified in ways that cause parts to work together, in parallel through the Laws of Similarities and Correspondence. Integrations of Concepts, Principles and Models working together. Elements are Interrelating and Interdependent without

Deviation or change as in Purpose of Action, Beginning, Forming Phase. Unity in physics is the unifying aspects of Naturally Integrating Systems, with a quality or state of being Multiple. Intent is the determination of the system the Inertia of the System, from the Beginning.

Concept: Something conceived in the mind, thoughts, motion.

Principles: Fundamental law, assumptions, laws or facts of nature and living the working of an artificial device (axion).

Similarities/Correspondence:

Concepts/Principles/Models:

Interrelated/Interdependent without Deviations or change of Purpose of action.

Take Time to change the Continuum of Natural Disorder which just occurs to Future. To change by Nature, Function and Condition must be changed.

In order to Transform you must change Function. Function is changed by:

1); Deleting

2); Inserting

3); Permutation

Integrate (Unity), the sense of right and wrong

$E=mc^2$

E/ Energy; Potential Difference =

m/ Mass

c/ Speed of Light

O (with a line through it) / Energy spent to respond,

X/ Times/ X=Position

The "S" Curve and the Worldview of era we are in.

Information Era                Knowledge Era                Wisdom Era

Nature: Structure, Patterns, Processes. Any Totality, whether man made or God made, consists of three different and separate Elements which then must work together based upon the Physics of Correspondence to function properly to make the Totality whole. Even the God Head consists of three separate Elements which must work together. There are specific laws upon which this must be for the three different Elements to correspond "as one". Every Element of Nature has its proper functions within the Totality of Nature itself. Every aspect of Nature has a Structure to it in which it is built upon in order to be what it is Structured to be. Upon this structure, there are specific Patterns that must be followed to have the end result of this aspect of Nature. There must also be Processes within the Structure and Patterns which must be followed. Man discovered this years ago for tornados, earthquakes, and many different aspects of Nature. Any Totality is based upon these principles.

Human Beings are a Totality, the Wholeness of being human is based upon this and other principles. If one aspect of our whole is not in tune with the whole, the whole is then at risk.

Study the list of Totalities and examine, consider, and question your own life in the different areas of Elements listed under any Totality you think you might need assistance in. The Totalities correspond with the different areas on the body map and therefore correspond with the different human senses. Natural man and his nature is organized. We do not have to tell our subconscious what to do or how to do it. In fact, it just functions the way God created it to function. Besides, it isn't the subconscious which causes us problems most of the time, it is our own conscious. The conscious is the very part of our brain that can and does Perceive, Evaluate, Judge and

Decide. This part of our brain is doing its patterns and processes based upon the way it was structured after our birth here on earth.

The World is composed of 2 different systems: Natural and Man-Made Systems.

Wholeness Model is made of 3 separate systems known as Elements and 1 Totality level.

Humans are Systems

Integration Systems; 4 types: Symbolic, Energetic, Whole Body, and Linguistic.

Humans are Open Systems. Open Systems Admit, Accept and Express feed back and have permeable and flexible boundaries.

Closed systems are addictive systems. Closed Systems are not Open to new feed back, data, information. In Nature, success is achieved through Self Organization. When a Closed System is in decline natural forces come into play. Their only goal is to eliminate or lift the restrictions that keep the system closed. Stability becomes dysfunctional in this process. A Closed System can only duplicate itself as closed systems create more closed systems.

Chaos is discontinuous and non-linear.

TIME: Time itself, is the measure of measurable period, during which an action, process, or condition exists or continues (Action, process, condition, exists or continues, continuum).

Time is non-spatial, and its continuum is measured in terms of the events which succeed one another from the past through the present and into the future. One of a series of recurring instances or repeated actions, added or accumulated quantities or instances. Finite to infinite duration. Time itself naturally is designed to cause actions, processes or conditions of the Future, to naturally turn to a state of Disorder. This is a very natural part of time as actions, processes or conditions must constantly change for Future movement. There are many aspects showing the way the Earth, Mankind, business, and life itself is constantly changing.

Time can actually be used itself to be a part of being able to change the continuum of Natural Disorder of Future Movements. This Natural Disorder is partly due to the unavailable energy in any Closed System and any System becomes a Closed System when it is not changing constantly between past, present, and future measurements, which is the meaning and Function of Time.

The Unavailable energy in a Closed System will vary directly with any reversible change depending upon the degree of disorder required for the degree of change for Future actions, processes, or conditions, within any given system.

Time is a measurement of events, actions, conditions, or processes that exist or continue.

Take Time to change the continuum of Natural Disorder of Future. Disorder is the unavailable energy in a closed system. This energy varies directly with any reversible change within the system; Degree of disorder (uncertainty in the system).

# Chapter 15

# EXCHANGE OF ENERGY IS DISCONTINUOUS

Disorder is the Natural process, involving the Entropy Cycle of unavailable energy due to its existence being denied, refused and repressed in the Closed System from the beginning. This Energy is existing in the System is unskilled (due to being denied, refused and repressed) and has been unavailable for the same reasons. This Entropy becomes anomalies to the Closed System, this Energy's Only Function is to eliminate or lift the restrictions keeping the System Closed.

The Energy of the Anomalies are an exchange of Energy and is therefore Discontinuous Energy. This Disorder is Reversible Disorder when the System is Open to Change.

Disorder and Uncertainty (Anomalies) relates directly to Function. Function is the purpose, the origin or originating of it all. Even though the Energy causing it existed since Forming Phase. Function is directly related to the Fulfilling or Success Phase. Fulfillment is the purpose.

Example of: ("This is my work and my glory to bring to pass the immortality and eternal life of man.").

Theory: The unskilled unavailable energy causing the Disorder Uncertainty (anomalies, both similar and deviating) since the Forming Phase pertains to the ultimate Fulfillment of the Success Phase of the whole system.

What potential at forming was there for the Fulfilling/Success Phase of the System?

Forming of a particular shape or mold into a certain state or after a particular model.

To model by instruction and discipline, an essential or basic Element of, to come into existence.

Form: The shape, structure of something as distinguished from its material. The essential nature of a thing as distinguished from it's matter, as an Idea; 1a. b: the component of a thing that determines it's kind, an established method of expression or proceeding, procedure according to rule.

Norm: Authoritative standard, Principle of action serving to guide, regulate proper and acceptable conduct, Patterns, widespread practices, measures, metric.

Fulfill: To make full, to put into effect, Execute, meet the requirements of, to bring to an end, convert into Reality, develop full potentialities of, to accomplish, achieve, attain.

1. Effect, Purpose, meaning, with meaning, essence follows a course, Power to overcome resistive influences, performance. In substance, perform, becomes the cause of to bring to pass. Put this into place in a specific position or relationship and bring into it a specified state or condition. Devote (oneself) to a specific activity, then create a condition or cause to perform action, express it and apply it, start it in motion, in places of opposition.

2. Reality: Quality or State of being Real, Totalities of things and events, neither derivative nor dependent but exists necessarily, state of actually existing.

2a Convert into Reality

2b  To bring from I belief, physical nature, condition into another. Change function to another for more affective utilization. Transform. Develop full.

3.  Execute, carry out fully, do all provided and required, carry out design, perform what is required, give validity to, perform, implement, see through.

4. 1) Develop, 2) Full 3) Potential. Set forth, make clear in details, make visible, work at the possibilities of, produce by deliberate effort over a period of time. Make active, promote growth of, make available and able, provide more opportunity for effective even growth by successive changes. Become gradually, manifest into being, and in development. Antonyms; condense, stunt.

Unavailable Unacknowledged, Unskilled E (energy) potential difference to put into effect, to Execute to "convert into "Reality" to "Develop" full potentialities of since the Forming Phase and already within the System itself since the Forming.

Inert Uniformity is the purpose of the Entropy Cycle. Disorder and Uncertainty brings the Inert Uniformity. When we are responding properly to the disorder and uncertainty the system as a whole may continue to grow. The unavailable, unskilled energy within the system from the beginning becomes a part of the whole system for continued progress.

Disorder: To disturb the regular or normal Functions of the system. To upset a system; A state of things having been mixed up. Confusion, to make disorder. Things fall apart. Do not progress forward, Entropy. Antonym of Entropy; Negentropy.

Uncertainty: A quality or state of being uncertain. Doubt, Skepticism, suspicion, mistrust a lack of sureness about someone or something. Uncertainty may range from falling short of certainty to an almost complete lack of conviction or knowledge esp. about an outcome or result. Doubt suggests uncertainty and inability to make a decision. Doubt, Skepticism and Mistrust are Natural man, or human frailties. These are not about the environment outside ourselves, but about the environment within. These are about us. Doubt suggest uncertainty: and inability within us to even make a decision. The world, someone, or something else in the world is not to blame. Doubt pertains to our own thought patterns, our past, our own choices of actions, not another's.

Skepticism: Is an unwillingness to believe without conclusive evidence. Suspicion stresses lack of faith in the truth, reality, fairness or reliability of something or someone. Once again, these, as is this whole book, disclosing the Holograph of you, your true inner being, as it has been programmed upon the earth. Your Natural man, which you may learn to overcome if you choose to. The gospel ordinances and principles, the commandments are not a test, they are the path to overcoming our own human frailties. They are the way to wholeness, to happiness, and to joy. Not just because of God's blessings, also because of His knowing our inner true self, our potential difference, our eternal abilities, our strengths, and our intelligence. Skepticism sounds so innocent, yet it is actually unwillingness to believe. Unless Conclusive evidence is given, there is no ability to believe. Faith is not a true attribute when skepticism is present.

Suspicion: Mistrust is built upon suspicion. In other words, without suspicion there would be no mistrust. The truth, reality, fairness or reliability in something or someone else lacks faith. Lacking faith in truth, lacking faith in reality, lacking faith in fairness or reliability. Truth does not need your faith. The truth is the truth, whether you have faith in it or not. God is God whether you have faith in Him or not. Reality doesn't need your faith to be reality. Fairness or reliability is still all they are with or without your faith. Who is it that is losing when you lack faith in these things? You! You are the person who looses when you lack faith and are struggling with suspicions. These are your suspicions. Truth, reality, and such is not affected because you lack faith. Antonym of Suspicion; Certainty and Determinism.

Entropy Cycle

Anomalies you experience in life are a direct reflection of your own inner strengths you have not yet recognized and trained. Tired of Endless change? Learn Systemic change. Change of Transformation and unpredictable Exponential change.

Making shifts in 1 or 2 behaviors, changing a significant belief, or a choice point is important but ultimately endless. The World View that develops these behaviors and attitudes keeps you recycling through endless layers of dysfunctional patterns.

Learn to change the System to Transform and attain Unpredictable, Exponential Change.

Make Identity Level Change and Shift Your Whole Worldview.

To Become

Unpredictability: Acclimated, unachieved, unacknowledged, unacted, unadapted, unaddressed, unadmired, and unafraid.

Systemic: Relating to or common to a System, as in affecting the whole system. Example: Supplying those parts of the body that receive blood through the aorta rather than through the pulmonary arteries.

Success/Quantity, "Exponent": Symbolized expression of the operation of ability to rise to Power.

Power "Exponential" Function: Relating to the Exponent, express by an exponential function, characterized by or being an extremely rapid increase in size or extent. Increase rapidly, Skyrocketing. The mathematical operation of raising Quantity to a Power. Also called Involution. This whole system of self-increase within any given system involves this mathematical structure of enfolding elements of one system in the same or other systems elements. The systems themselves can more easily interact with each based upon the similar elements (data).

Involution: The act or an instance of enfolding or entangling (Involvement). Exponential complexity creates an inward curvature or penetration.

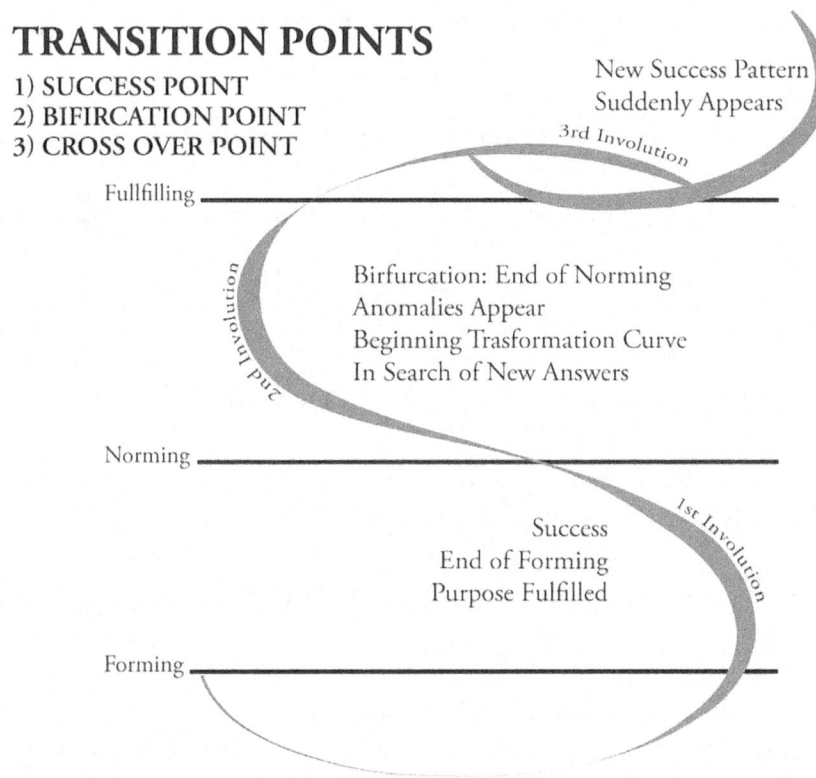

The Self view's Power and Exponential Function, (relating to the Exponent, express by an exponential function, characterized by or being an extremely rapid increase in size or extent), directly related to the World's view Quantity and Exponent (Quantity, "Exponent" Symbolized expression of the operation of ability to rise to Power) does an inward curve into the Success side of the Entropy Cycle. The Exponent is unidentified without the Exponential Function of the Self view.

Today Change itself has Changed. This has thrown our lives into turbulence. Facing all life's changes themselves has become such a great challenge that we have become lost in even facing the change.

Why is there always an even load? to any Success? This happens because all acts, processes, or instances have limits at their origin or beginnings. Origin implies (applies) to the things or persons from which something is ultimately derived and often to the cause operating before the thing itself came into Being.

"Inception" stresses the beginning of something without implying cause.

"Root" suggests a first, ultimate or fundamental source often not easily discerned.

To "Transform" you must change Function.

Changing Function attains Discontinuous Disorder.

Discontinuous: Not continuous, not continued, lacking sequence or coherence, used of a variable or a Function.

Disorder: To disturb the order of, to disturb the regular or normal Function of.

Anomalies, the Entropy Cycle creates the opportunity for Systemic changes. This is called Second Order Change. Second Order Change is Transformative and unpredictable Exponential change.

The Entropy Cycle designate by the letter S. This cycle has always been considered just a fact "and that's the way it is" as use to be stated by Walter Cronkite. This is not the case, once we understand a thing, we may also overcome the thing. The Entropy cycle from the Holographic Human Transformation Theory states that the Entropy is one of the Models of Transformation. In order to transform a thing, you must truly understand the micro and the macro as one. You must understand the function of each micro aspect as it pertains to the function of the macro (whole purpose).

The Entropy from a Transformation perception represents continued success and progression. Holographic Human Transformation Theory states that transforming the Entropy cycle brings about Discontinuous Disorder and

Discontinuous Uncertainty. Holographic Human Transformation Theory states that once all of the unavailable, unskilled, unrecognized energy (potential difference) is recognized, skilled, and available within the system for its function in the system, a whole new Entropy begins for continued success, progression, and growth with a whole new function and purpose with new potential differences. Continued growth, continued potential, Disorder and Uncertainty in our lives being Discontinuous instead of Continuous, New Beginnings for our continued growth Just appearing in our lives as we progress forward.

The reason of this being that we understand the Disorder and Uncertainty as we grow and progress, we recognize it as coming from within our own system and having a vital purpose of Potential difference for Success within the system. We are able to know the area within us where the potential difference resides, and we have a map or guide to assist us in seeing this clearly on a conscious level.

The Holographic Human Map, which is the Map of our own Micro and Macro Functions for our own Whole Purpose, laid on the S curve, the Entropy Cycle, in our individual firing order through our senses, shows the specific sense the unavailable, unskilled, energy is. Again, this is real potential within the system itself. This real energy has a real Function within the System within ourselves. This Energy does not just go away, nor does it even dissipate, it is continuous Energy, and it will continue to do everything it is trained or skilled to do to get the Macro, the Whole system, the Whole You to recognize it. It is of course not trained, nor skilled as to what it's Function is, so it's negative will come out. This will happen until the Macro, You, recognize it. Recognize the Potential Difference within you, and You change. Your Functions and your Purpose change.

The first 3 senses fired are your World View Beliefs. Your last 3 senses fired are your Self View Beliefs. Your World View Beliefs must change in order for your Self View Beliefs to stop recycling through their dysfunctional patterns. Your World View and Your Self View Beliefs should work in parallel with one another, resolving together their own Disorders and Uncertainties.

50% of the Data the subconscious has to create our Models, Programs, our Personality, Identity, and Beliefs is nothing more than sensory data. This sensory data is based upon our sense of sight, sound, energy, touch, smell, and taste. This is the Data the subconscious has and uses to process and put together for our automatic subconscious structure, patterns, and processes.

Listening to another's Worldview (which keeps Self view recycling through dysfunctional patterns), doesn't change Worldview (nor Self view). It may comfort a person at the time to "Express" it, to hear kind words in return but ultimately will be an endless process of layer upon layer of Self dysfunctional patterns.

Self view is the "Power and the Exponential Function of the Worldview. The mathematical function in which an independent variable appears in one of the exponents. Also called exponential. Of or relating to an exponent. Involving a variable in an exponent (10x is an exponential expression). Expressible or approximately expressible by an exponential function. Especially characterized by or being an extremely rapid increase (as in the size or extent). Such as an exponential growth rate. Increasing rapidly, skyrocketing, exponential, surging. Antonym; plummeting. Of various rates Of growth. IE: Constant, linear, polynomial; exponential.

Process/Technique: Create a questioning process from Self views "relating" Sense to use in response to their "Expressing" "Worldview". Based upon an individual's sensory firing order, different senses and their models and programs will create different World and Self views. As the Entropy Cycle function today, with the World view and Self view not recognizing one another, we continue to plummet, even though we can succeed.

It is true that life does have ups and downs. It is not true that intelligent living beings have no say nor effect on the ups and downs of life. Mankind nor intelligence is an Entropy Cycle. Different theories theorize different concepts, still the one known fact is this: Living intelligent human beings is all we have known for a fact we have ever known us to come from upon this earth. Even test tube is traced back to us. Man-made systems such as Walmart or McDonalds have survived the Entropy's cycle plummet certainly mankind whether as individuals or as a holographic whole can also survive the Entropy plummet.

NEGENTROPY

Negentropy is the antonym of Entropy. Negentropy is created by integrating any Disorder and Uncertainty in any given System into the System. Disorder and Uncertainty is a direct result of any anomalies arising in the System. Negentropy happens when the system recognizes, acknowledges and trains the energy causing the anomalies and Disorder and Uncertainty. Uncertainty within the System specifically refers to the System's own areas of Doubt, skepticisms; Mistrust implies a genuine Doubt based upon Suspicions. In an Open System this energy becomes a welcome part of the Systems Functions and Potential.

This is a process of integration, of taking Inter-related, Inter-dependent Elements of a Whole Systems and having them work together for the Whole of the System. 1) Be certain and make a Decision, 2) Be willing to believe without conclusive evidence, have faith in the truth, reality, fairness and reliability of something or someone, 3) Trust Choice, based upon faith in truth, reality, fairness and reliability. Identify the Inter-related, Inter-dependent Elements within your own System and Become a Negentropy, Open System.

Wholeness is the Principle intent Anomalies naturally work to achieve. Wholeness is The Unifying Force which holds us together, inner unification comes from the macro-system to live and grow. What we resist persists. This force promotes Integration of all parts. Integrate, exists because of structure, patterns and processes. Natural Systems are unified in ways that cause parts to work together, in parallel, through the Laws of Similarities and Correspondence. Integrations of Concepts, Principles and Models working together to make them Inter-related and Inter-dependent.

Elements are Interrelating and Interdependent without Deviation or change as in Purpose of Action, each Element maintaining it's own Identity, its structures, patterns and process it exists for.

Unity in physics is the unifying aspects of Naturally Integrating Systems, with a quality or state of being Multiple.

Intent is the determination of the system, the Inertia of the System, from the Beginning.

Worldview is the structure, patterns and processes the System is viewing the World or Environment through regarding the Success of the Whole System. The Worldview is created through the first 3 senses fired in your Personality firing order. This is also the Exponent of the Whole System. It is also the Quantity of the Success of the Whole System.

Self-view is created through the last 3 senses fired in your Personality firing order. This is and Power and Exponential FUNCTION for the Worldview.

In order to Transform you must change Function. Function is changed by:

1); Deleting

2); Inserting

3); Permutation

Integrate (Unity), the sense of right and wrong

Integration: Integrated Systems: Elements and Function are interrelated and interdependent upon other Elements and Function. Changing one Element of an Integrated System affects the rest of the system entirety. Integration is the process of making Whole and this works due to Correspondence, Unity, Reality and Wholeness Principles.

Systemic; relating to or common to a System, as in affecting the whole system. Ex; supplying those parts of the body that receive blood through the aorta rather than through the pulmonary arteries.

Success/Quantity "Exponent": Symbolized expression of the operation of ability to rise to Power.

Power: "Exponential" Function, relating to the Exponent, expressed by an exponential function, characterized by or being an extremely rapid increase in size or extent. Increase rapidly, SKYROCKETING…

The mathematical operation of raising Quantity to a Power, called also, involution.

Involution: The act or an instance of enfolding or entangling: (Involvement). Exponential, complexity. An inward curvature or penetration.

The Self view's Power and Exponential Function, directly related to the World's view Quantity and Exponent does an inward curve into the Success side of the Entropy Cycle. The Exponent is unidentified without the Exponential Function of the Self view.

Today Change itself has Changed. This has thrown our lives into turbulence. Facing all life's changes themselves has become such a great challenge that we have become lost in even facing the change.

Why is there always an even load, to any Success? This happens because all acts, processes, or instances have limits at their origin or beginnings. Origin implies (applies) to the things or persons from which something is ultimately derived and often to the cause operating Before the thing itself came into Being. "Inception" stresses the beginning of something without implying cause. "Root" suggests a first, ultimate or fundamental source often not easily discerned.

To Transform you must change Function. Changing Function attains Discontinuous Disorder.

Anomalies and the Entropy Cycle creates the opportunity for Systemic changes. This is called Second Order Change. Second Order Change is Transformative and unpredictable Exponential change.

MATH

E times 10, raised to an indicated exponent.

N, unspecified symbol as an exponent

Self-view is the "Power and the Exponential Function of the

Worldview.

Negentropy turns Disorder and Uncertainty into Discontinuous Disorder and Uncertainty. It doesn't just disappear to never return still it is Welcomed and Skilled into the Whole System and becomes Discontinuous.

The Worldview must change in order for the Self View to stop recycling through its dysfunctional patterns and Self View must change in order for World View to change.

Integrating the 2 views in an Inter-related, Inter-dependent manner causes both views to change independently-together.

Example of this: the sense of touch, the elements, theories, questions and take no action. Many of us instead, take action when we are emotional in the present. Stop communicating and do not create dialogues of the situation nor new theories to apply.

# Chapter 16

# "S" Curve

First is Forming: Explore possibilities until success patterns are discovered or invented.

Second is Norming: The Success Patterns are repeated over and over.

Third is Fulfilling: "S" Curve begins to flatten a bit still rising, growth is now achieved by integrating differences and modifications into the original pattern. The system reaches it's peak then begins to decline, having attained it fullest possible expression.

Incremental Change is Endless, small shifts in behaviors

Transformative Change is unpredictable Change and exponential Change. This represents an Identity Level Change.

Structure of Transformation

To change by Nature, Function, condition.

3 Transition Points: 1); Success Point, 2) Bifurcation Point, 3): Cross Over Point.

1): Success: End of Forming Phase, fulfilled purpose.

2): Bifurcation Point: End of Norming Phase, Anomalies appear. The beginning of The Transformation Curve. (In search of New Answers).

3): Cross Over Point: A new Success Pattern will suddenly appear, (Discontinuity). Jumping the Curve, the Change Curve.

1): The Age/Era of Integrity

2): The Age/Era of Light

Doing Things Right. Doing Right Things.

Only the Whole System can fly.

Educate means to Draw out not to Pour In.

1): Unique qualities, talents of each.

2): A sense of commonality between the individual and their environment, the common thread they have with each other and a bond with the natural world.

3): A balancing and harmonizing of unique individuality with a sense of commonality.

Human Beings have characteristics and attributes representative of frailties, sympathies, and strengths, and by nature of their minds can process and evaluate their lives and many other things. They have a conscious existence and may perceive and conceive other things into real existence.

In order to Transform, the key of the formula affecting Transformation is FUNCTION. Function is the literal operation that converts one thing into another. Function is changed by doing any or all of the following: Deleting, Inserting, or Permutation. Deleting is the first element, inserting is the second element, and permutation is the third element of transformation. Transform Function using any or all of the mentioned elements. Integration is a process of unifying (Unity). Humans Transform and Integrate by nature. Their inherent sense of right and wrong, in accordance with and determined by their very nature. Adam and Eve ate the apple, the tree of knowledge of right and wrong and good and evil. They became mortal, we are their offspring. We are born into mortality knowing right from wrong and good from evil. This knowledge is programmed into our being. This sense affects other programs of our being. Inert uniformity is a response of this knowledge. Closed Systems, Entropy, Correspondence, it all functions around the tree of knowledge. Permutation is major and fundamental change (as in a character or condition), based primarily on rearrangement of existent elements. Changing by the act or process, the lineal order of and ordered set or arrangements of character or conditions.

A Quantum Leap is an abrupt Transition (as of an electron, an atom, molecule) from one discrete energy state to another. Identity and sameness of essential or genetic character in different instances. Sameness in all that constitutes the objective reality of a thing. A quality whose effect is to leave the multiplied unchanged (The number that is to be multiplied by another). The being remains the being, though character and condition may change. The goal remains the goal, objective remains the objective while character and condition of goal and objective may change.

Communication being a process by which information is exchanged between individuals through a common system of symbols, signs or behaviors, exchange of information.

Communication: The act or process of transferring Data.

Healing Model: 2 approaches: 1) Physical, 2): Spiritual.

1): Physical= Nutrition, Fitness, Hygiene Body Maintenance

2): Spiritual= Body System Matrix, Belief Integration, Addictive Systems (Closed), Energy System.

Language of emotions as they relate to the Holographic Human Model.

Innocence: In No Sense. Innocence breeds more Innocence.

Humiliation is the ultimate strategy of limitation.

Striving to attain a state of innocence is about Knowing Thy Self and being Thy Self regardless of life circumstances. Innocence is not about naivety, it is about being open to the feedback in your environment. Innocence in not becoming dysfunctional, it is expanding on your being amid life's circumstances that you can't control.

Properties and characteristics of our natural being need not be formed or added onto, only expanded. The Inner World of Being is different than the Outer World of Doing. Human Beings are good and deserving by Nature.

Models-forming internal representations of our experiences. A Model is not a Memory, it is a collection of Memories. PARADIGMS (Programs in the Human Subconscious).

Algorithm of Elements of Holographic Human Transformation Theory

(SIMILIARS)Mind-emotion-body-Identity-communicate-create-Father-mother-child-Natural-systems-elements-Conscious-subconscious-limbic-Reference-decision-motivator-Delete-distort-generalize-Structure-patterns-processes-Space-time-matter-Past-present-future- Data-information-model-Symbolic-energetic-whole body-data-information-knowledge-Delete-distort-generalize-Data-processing-information-Data-dialogue-knowledge-Reception-storage-transmits-Direction-question-model-Action-no action-let others take action-Patterns-programs and models-Intent-context-content-Data-information-feedback-Receive-storage-transmission-Transmit-receive-message-Intent-context-content-Symbols-letters-numbers-Musc notes-senses-pictures- Sympathies-frailties-strengths-Hope-faith-charity-Shifts in programs-models-beliefs-Height-Lateral-Depth-Space-enviornment-self-Nutrition- fitness-hygiene-Body system-belief -integration-

Sound and Sight

(SIMILIARS)Mind-emotion-mind-body-mind-Identity-communicate-identity-create-identity-Father-mother-father-child-father-Natural-systems-natural-elements-natual-Conscious

-subconscious-conscious-limbic-conscious-Reference-decision-reference-motivator-reference-Structure-patterns-structure-processes-structue-Space-time-space-matter-space-Past-present-past-future-past-Data-information-data-model-data-Symbolic-energetic-symbolic-whole body-symbolic-Data-information-data-knowledge-data-Delete-distort-delete-generalize-delete-Data-processing-data-information-data-Data-dialogue-data-knowledge-data-Reception-storage-reception-transmits-reception-Direction-question-direction-model-direction-Action-no action-action-let others take action-action-Patterns-programs-patterns and models-patterns-Intent-context-intent-content-intent-Data-information-data-feedback-data-Receive-storage-receive-transmission-receive-Transmit-receive-transmit-message-transmit-Intent-context-intent-content-intent-Symbols-letters-symbols-numbers-symbols-Music notes-senses-music notes-pictures-music notes- Sympathies-frailties-sympathies-strengths-sympathies-Hope-faith-hope-charity-hope-Shifts in programs-models-shifts-beliefs-shifts-Height-Lateral-height-Depth-heght-Space-enviornment-space-self-space-Nutrition-fitness-nutrition-hygiene-nutrtion-Body system-belief-body-integration-body

Touch and Energy

(SIMILIARS)Mind-emotion-emotion-body-emotion-Identity-communicate-communicate-create-commuicate-Father-mother-mother-child-mother-Natural-systems-systems-elements-systems-Conscious-subconscious-subconscious-limbic-subconscious-Reference-decision-decision-motivator-decision-Structure-patterns-patterns-processes-patterns-Space-time-tme-matter-tme-Past-present-present-future-prsent-Data-information-information-model-information-Symbolic-energetic-energetic-whole body-energetic-data-information-information-knowledge-informtion-Delete-distort-distort-generalize-distort-Data-processing-processing-information-processing- -Data-dialogue-dialogue-knowledge-dialogue-Reception-storage-storage-transmits-storage-Direction-question-

question-model-question- Action-no, action-no action-let others take action-no action-Patterns-programs-programs-models-programs-Intent-context-context-content-context-Data-information-information-feedback-information-Receive-storage-storage-transmission-storage-Transmit-receive-receive-message-receive-Symbols-letters-letters-numbers-letters-Musc notes-senses-senses-pictures-senses-Sympathies-frailies-frailties-strengths-frailties-Hope-faith-faith-charity-faith-Shifts in programs-models-models-beliefs-models-Height-lateral-Lateral-Depth-lateral-Space-enviornment-enviornment-self-enviornment-Nutrition-fitness-fitness-hygiene-fitness-Body system-belief-belief-integration-belief

Taste and Smell

(SIMILIARS)Mind-body-emotion-body-body-Identity-create-communicate-create-create-Father-child-mother-child-child-Natural-elements-systems-elements-elements-Conscious-limbic-subconscious-limbic-limbic-Reference-moivator-decision-motivator-motivator-Structure-processes-patterns-processes-processes-Space-matter-time-matter-matter-Past-future-present-future-future-Data-model-information-model-model-Symbolic-whole body-energetic-whole body-whole body-Data-knowledge-information-knowledge-knowledge-Delete-generalize-distort-generalize-generalize-Data-information-processing-information-information-Data-knowledge-dialogue-knowledge-knowledge-Reception-transmits-storage-transmits-transmits-Direction-model-question-model-model-Action-let others take action-no action-let others take action-let others take action-Patterns-models-programs-models-models-Intent-content-context-content-content-Data-feedback-information-feedback-feedback-Receive-transmission-storage-transmission-transmission-Transmit-message-receive-message-message-Intent-content-context-content-content-Symbols-numbers-letters-numbers-numbers-Musc notes-pictures-senses-pictures-pictures- Sympathies-strengths-frailties-strengths-strengths-Hope-charity-faith-charity-charity-Shifts in programs-beliefs-models-beliefs-beliefs-Height-depth-Lateral-depth-Depth-Space-self-enviornment-self-self-Nutrition-hygiene-fitness-hygiene-hygiene-Body system-integration-belief-integration-integration-

(UNITY/DEVIATING) Deny-refuse-repress- Unacknowledged-unavailable-untrained- Doubt-uncertainty limiting beliefs-Similar-deviating-randomness disorder-Action-function-process-Hopeless-helpless-worthless-Stability-chaos-randomness disorder-Integration-reality-data processing-Fear-shame-guilt-

Sound and Sight

(UNITY/DEVIATING) Deny-refuse-deny-repress-deny-Unacknowledged-unavailable-unacknowledged-untrained-unacknowledged-Doubt-uncertainty-doubt-limiting beliefs-doubt-Similar-deviating-similar-randomness disorder-similiar-Action-function-action-process-action-Hopeless-helpless-hopeless-worthless-helpless-Stability-chaos-stability-randomness disorder-stability-Integration-reality-integration-data processing-integration-Fear-shame-fear-guilt-fear

Touch and Energy

(UNITY/DEVIATING) Deny-refuse-refuse-repress-refuse-Unacknowledged-unavailable-unavailable-untrained-unavailable- Doubt-uncertainty-uncertainty-limiting beliefs-uncertainty-Similar-deviating-deviating-randomness disorder-deviatng-Action-function-function-process-function-Hopeless-helpless-helpless-worthless-helpless-Stability-chaos-chaos-randomness disorder-chaos-Integration-reality-reality-data processing-reality-Fear-shame-shame-guilt-shame

Taste and Smell

(UNITY/DEVIATING) Deny-repress-refuse-repress-repress-Unacknowledged-untrained-unavailable-untrained-untrained-Doubt-limitig beliefs-uncertainty-limiting beliefs-limiting beliefs-Similar-randomness disorder-deviating-randomness disorder-randomness disorder-Action-process-function-process-process-Hopeless-worthless-helpless-worthless-worthless-Stability-randomness disorder-chaos-randomness disorder-randomness disorder-Integration-data processing-reality-data processing-data processing-Fear-guilt-shame-guilt-guilt-

(INTEGRATING) Admit-accept-express-Form-norm-fulfill-Success point-bifurcation point-cross over point-Delete-insert-permutate-Similar-unity-integrate-Natural disorder-discontinuous disorder-unpredictable identity- Wholeness-totality-correspondence-Models-processes-beliefs-Integration-concepts-principles-Success patterns-extend patterns-considering anomalies-Nature-function-condition-Outcome-condition-state-

Sound and Sight

(INTEGRATING) Admit-accept-admit-express-admit-Form-norm-form-fulfill-form-Success point-bifurcation point-success point-cross over point-success point-Delete-insert-delete-permutate-delete-Similar-unity-similiar-integrate-similar-Natural disorder-discontinuous disorder-natural disorder-unpredictable identity-natural disorder-Wholeness-totality-wholeness-correspondence-wholeness-Models-processes-models-beliefs-models-Integration-concepts-integretion-principles-integration-Success patterns-extend patterns-success patterns-considering anomalies-success patterns-Nature-function-nature-condition-nature-Outcome-condition-outcome-state-outcome

Touch and Energy

(INTEGRATING) Admit-accept-accept-express-accept-Form-norm-norm-fulfill-norm-Success point-bifurcation point—bifurcation point-cross over point-bifurcation point-Delete-insert-insert-permutate-insert-Similar-unity-unity-integrate-unity-Natural disorder-discontinuous disorder-discontinuous disorder-unpredictable identity-discontinuous disorder- Wholeness-totality-totality-correspondence-totality-Models-processes-processes-beliefs-processes-Integration-concepts-concepts-principles-concepts-Success patterns-extended patterns-extend patterns-considering anomalies-extended patterns-Nature-function-function-condition-function-Outcome-condition-condition-state-condition-

Taste and Smell

(INTEGRATING) Admit-express-accept-express-express-Form-fulfill-norm-fulfill-fulfill-Success point-cross over point-bifurcation point-cross over point-cross over point-Delete-permutate-insert-permutate-permutate-Similar-integrate-unity-integrate-integrate-Natural disorder-unpredictable identity-discontinuous disorder-unpredictable identity-unpredictable identity- Wholeness-correspondence-totality-correspondence-correspondence-Models-beliefs-processes-beliefs-beliefs-Integration-principles-concepts-principles-principles-Success patterns-considering anomalies-extend patterns-considering anomalies-considering anomalies-Nature-condition-function-condition-condition-Outcome-state-condition-state-state-

## ALGORITHYMS SEQUENCED AND CORRESPONDING TO SENSES

Sound and Sight Add first element to the other 2 elements per totality set)

(SIMILIARS)Mind-emotion-mind-body-mind-Identity-communicate-identity-create-identity-Father-mother-father-child-father-Natural-systems-natural-elements-natual-Conscious-subconscious-conscious-limbic-conscious-Reference-decision-reference-motivator-reference-Structure-patterns-structure-processes-structue-Space-time-space-matter-space-Past-present-past-future-past-Data-information-data-model-data-Symbolic-energetic-symbolic-whole body-symbolic-Data-information-data-knowledge-data-Delete-distort-delete-generalize-delete-Data-processing-data-information-data-Data-dialogue-data-knowledge-data-Reception-storage-reception-transmits-reception-Direction-question-direction-model-direction-Action-no action-action-let others take action-action-Patterns-programs-patterns and models-patterns-Intent-context-intent-content-intent-Data-information-data-feedback-data-Receive-storage-receive-transmission-receive-Transmit-receive-transmit-message-transmit-Intent-context-intent-content-intent-Symbols-letters-symbols-numbers-symbols-Music notes-senses-music notes-pictures-music notes- Sympathies-frailties-sympathies-strengths-sympathies-Hope-faith-hope-charity-hope-Shifts in programs-models-shifts-beliefs-shifts-Height-Lateral-height-Depth-heght-Space-enviornment-space-self-space-Nutrition-fitness-nutrition-hygiene-nutrtion-Body system-belief-body-integration-body

Sound and Sight

(UNITY/DEVIATING) Deny-refuse-deny-repress-deny-Unacknowledged-unavailable-unacknowledged-untrained-unacknowledged-Doubt-uncertainty-doubt-limiting beliefs-doubt-Similar-deviating-similar-randomness disorder-similiar-Action-function-action-process-action-Hopeless-helpless-hopeless-worthless-helpless-Stability-chaos-stability-randomness disorder-stability-Integration-reality-integration-data processing-integration-Fear-shame-fear-guilt-fear

Sound and Sight

(INTEGRATING) Admit-accept-admit-express-admit-Form-norm-form-fulfill-form-Success point-bifurcation point-success point-cross over point-success point-Delete-insert-delete-permutate-delete-Similar-unity-similiar-integrate-similar-Natural disorder-discontinuous disorder-natural disorder-unpredictable identity-natural disorder-Wholeness-totality-wholeness-correspondence-wholeness-Models-processes-models-beliefs-models-Integration-concepts-integretion-principles-integration-Success patterns-extend patterns-success patterns-considering anomalies-success patterns-Nature-function-nature-condition-nature-Outcome-condition-outcome-state-outcome

Touch and Energy (Add second element of to the other 2 elements in the set)

(SIMILIARS)Mind emotion-emotion-body emotion-Identity-communicate-communicate-create-commuicate-Father-mother-mother-child-mother-Natural-systems-systems-elements-systems-Conscious-subconscious-subconscious-limbic-subconscious-Reference-decision-decision-motivator-decision-Structure-patterns-patterns-processes-patterns-Space-time-tme-matter-tme-Past-present-present-future-prsent-Data-information-information-model-information-Symbolic-energetic-energetic-whole body-energetic-data-information-information-knowledge-informtion-Delete-distort-distort-generalize-distort-Data-processing-processing-information-processing- -Data-dialogue-dialogue-knowledge-dialogue-Reception-storage-storage-transmits-storage-Direction-question-question-model-question- Action-no action-no action-let others take action-no action-Patterns-programs-programs-models-programs-Intent-context-context-content-context-Data-information-information-feedback-information-Receive-storage-storage-transmission-storage-Transmit-receive-receive-message-receive-Symbols-letters-letters-numbers-letters-Musc notes-senses-senses-pictures-senses-Sympathies-frailies-frailties-strengths-frailties-Hope-faith-faith-charity-faith-Shifts in programs-models-models-beliefs-models-Height-lateral-Lateral-Depth-lateral-Space-enviornment-enviornment-self-enviornment-Nutrition-fitness-fitness-hygiene-fitness-Body system-belief-belief-integration-belief

Touch and Energy

(UNITY/DEVIATING) Deny-refuse-refuse-repress-refuse-Unacknowledged-unavailable-unavailable-untrained-unavailable- Doubt-uncertainty-uncertainty-limiting beliefs-uncertainty-Similar-deviating-deviating-randomness disorder-deviatng-Action-function-function-process-function-Hopeless-helpless-helpless-worthless-helpless-Stability-chaos-chaos-randomness disorder-chaos-Integration-reality-reality-data processing-reality-Fear-shame-shame-guilt-shame

Touch and Energy

(INTEGRATING) Admit-accept-accept-express-accept-Form-norm-norm-fulfill-norm-Success point-bifurcation point—bifurcation point-cross over point-bifurcation point-Delete-insert-insert-permutate-insert-Similar-unity-unity-integrate-unity-Natural disorder-discontinuous disorder-discontinuous disorder-unpredictable identity-discontinuous disorder- Wholeness-totality-totality-correspondence-totality-Models-processes-processes-beliefs-processes-Integration-concepts-concepts-principles-concepts-Success patterns-extended patterns-extend patterns-considering anomalies-extended patterns-Nature-function-function-condition-function-Outcome-condition-condition-state-condition-

Taste and Smell (Add third element of each element to the other 2 elements of the same set)

(SIMILIARS)Mind body-emotion body-body-Identity create-communicate create-create-Father-child-mother-child-child-Natural-elements-systems-elements-elements-Conscious-limbic-subconscious-limbic-limbic-Reference-moivator-decision-motivator-motivator-Structure-processes-patterns-processes-processes-Space-matter-time-matter-matter-Past-future-present-future-future-Data-model-information-model-model-Symbolic-whole body-energetic-whole body-whole body-Data-knowledge-information-knowledge-knowledge-Delete-generalize-distort-generalize-generalize-Data-information-processing-information-information-Data-knowledge-dialogue-knowledge-knowledge-Reception-transmits-storage-transmits-transmits-Direction-model-question-model-model-Action-let others take action-no action-let others take action-let others take action-Patterns-models-programs-models-models-Intent-content-context-content-content-Data-feedback-information-feedback-feedback-Receive-transmission-storage-transmission-transmission-Transmit-message-receive-message-message-Intent-content-context-content-content-Symbols-nembers-letters-numbers-numbers-Musc notes-pictures-senses-pictures-pictures- Sympathies-strengths-frailties-strengths-strengths-Hope-charity-faith-charity-charity-Shifts in programs-beliefs-models-beliefs-beliefs-Height-depth-Lateral-depth-Depth-Space-self-enviornment-self-self-Nutrition-hygiene-fitness-hygiene-hygiene-Body system-integration-belief-integration-integration-

Taste and Smell

(UNITY/DEVIATING) Deny-repress-refuse-repress-repress-Unacknowledged-untrained-unavailable-untrained-untrained-Doubt-limitig beliefs-uncertainty-limiting beliefs-limiting beliefs-Similar-randomness disorder-deviating-randomness disorder-randomness disorder-Action-process-function-process-process-Hopeless-worthless-helpless-worthless-worthless-Stability-randomness disorder-chaos-randomness disorder-randomness disorder-Integration-data processing-reality-data processing-data processing-Fear-guilt-shame-guilt-guilt-

Taste and Smell

(INTEGRATING) Admit-express-accept-express-express-Form-fulfill-norm-fulfill-fulfill-Success point-cross over point-bifurcation point-cross over point-cross over point-Delete-permutate-insert-permutate-permutate-Similar-integrate-unity-integrate-integrate-Natural disorder-unpredictable identity-discontinuous disorder-unpredictable identity-unpredictable identity- Wholeness-correspondence-totality-correspondence-correspondence-Models-beliefs-processes-beliefs-beliefs-Integration-principles-concepts-principles-principles-Success patterns-considering anomalies-extend patterns-considering anomalies-considering anomalies-Nature-condition-function-condition-condition-Outcome-state-condition-state-state-

# SOUND

(SIMILIARS)Mind-emotion mind body mind-Identity-communicate-identity-create identity-Father-mother-father child-father-Natural systems-natural elements-natural-Conscious subconscious-conscious-limbic-conscious-Reference-decision-reference-motivator-reference-Structure-patterns-structure-processes-structue-Space-time-space-matter-space-Past-present-past-future-past-Data-information-data-model-data-Symbolic-energetic-symbolic-whole body-symbolic-Data-information-data-knowledge-data-Delete-distort-delete-generalize-delete-Data-processing-data-information-data-Data-dialogue-data-knowledge-data-Reception-storage-reception-transmits-reception-Direction-question-direction-model-direction-Action-no action-action-let others take action-action-Patterns-programs-patterns and models-patterns-Intent-context-intent-content-intent-Data-information-data-feedback-data-Receive-storage-receive-transmission-receive-Transmit-receive-transmit-message-transmit-Intent-context-intent-content-intent-Symbols-letters-symbols-numbers-symbols-Music notes-senses-music notes-pictures-music notes- Sympathies-frailties-sympathies-strengths-sympathies-Hope-faith-hope-charity-hope-Shifts in programs-models-shifts-beliefs-shifts-Height-Lateral-height-Depth-heght-Space-enviornment-space-self-space-Nutrition-fitness-nutrition-hygiene-nutrtion-Body system-belief-body-integration-body

(UNITY/DEVIATING) Deny-refuse-deny-repress-deny-Unacknowledged-unavailable-unacknowledged-untrained-unacknowledged-Doubt-uncertainty-doubt-limiting beliefs-doubt-Similar-deviating-similar-randomness disorder-similiar-Action-function-action-process-action-Hopeless-helpless-hopeless-worthless-helpless-Stability-chaos-stability-randomness disorder-stability-Integration-reality-integration-data processing-integration-Fear-shame-fear-guilt-fear

(INTEGRATING) Admit-accept-admit-express-admit-Form-norm-form-fulfill-form-Success point-bifurcation point-success point-cross over point-success point-Delete-insert-delete-permutate-delete-Similar-unity-similiar-integrate-similar-Natural disorder-discontinuous disorder-natural disorder-unpredictable identity-natural disorder-Wholeness-totality-wholeness-correspondence-wholeness-Models-processes-models-beliefs-models-Integration-concepts-integretion-principles-integration-Success patterns-extend patterns-success patterns-considering anomalies-success patterns-Nature-function-nature-condition-nature-Outcome-condition-outcome-state-outcome

# SIGHT

(SIMILIARS)Mind-emotion-mind-body-mind-Identity-communicate-identity-create-identity-Father-mother-father-child-father-Natural-systems-natural-elements-natual-Conscious-subconscious-conscious-limbic-conscious-Reference-decision-reference-motivator-reference-Structure-patterns-structure-processes-structue-Space-time-space-matter-space-Past-present-past-future-past-Data-information-data-model-data-Symbolic-energetic-symbolic-whole body-symbolic-Data-information-data-knowledge-data-Delete-distort-delete-generalize-delete-Data-processing-data-information-data-Data-dialogue-data-knowledge-data-Reception-storage-reception-transmits-reception-Direction-question-direction-model-direction-Action-no action-action-let others take action-action-Patterns-programs-patterns and models-patterns-Intent-context-intent-content-intent-Data-information-data-feedback-data-Receive-storage-receive-transmission-receive-Transmit-receive-transmit-message-transmit-Intent-context-intent-content-intent-Symbols-letters-symbols-numbers-symbols-Music notes-senses-music notes-pictures-music notes- Sympathies-frailties-sympathies-strengths-sympathies-Hope-faith-hope-charity-hope-Shifts in programs-models-shifts-beliefs-shifts-Height-Lateral-height-Depth-heght-Space-enviornment-space-self-space-Nutrition-fitness-nutrition-hygiene-nutrtion-Body system-belief-body-integration-body

(UNITY/DEVIATING) Deny-refuse-deny-repress-deny-Unacknowledged-unavailable-unacknowledged-untrained-unacknowledged-Doubt-uncertainty-doubt-limiting beliefs-doubt-Similar-deviating-similar-randomness disorder-similiar-Action-function-action-process-action-Hopeless-helpless-hopeless-worthless-helpless-Stability-chaos-stability-randomness disorder-stability-Integration-reality-integration-data processing-integration-Fear-shame-fear-guilt-fear

(INTEGRATING) Admit-accept-admit-express-admit-Form-norm-form-fulfill-form-Success point-bifurcation point-success point-cross over point-success point-Delete-insert-delete-permutate-delete-Similar-unity-similiar-integrate-similar-Natural disorder-discontinuous disorder-natural disorder-unpredictable identity-natural disorder-Wholeness-totality-wholeness-correspondence-wholeness-Models-processes-models-beliefs-models-Integration-concepts-integretion-principles-integration-Success patterns-extend patterns-success patterns-considering anomalies-success patterns-Nature-function-nature-condition-nature-Outcome-condition-outcome-state-outcome

# TOUCH

(SIMILIARS)Mind-emotion-mind-body-mind-Identity-communicate-identity-create-identity-Father-mother-father-child-father-Natural-systems-natural-elements-natual-Conscious-subconscious-conscious-limbic-conscious-Reference-decision-reference-motivator-reference-Structure-patterns-structure-processes-structue-Space-time-space-matter-space-Past-present-past-future-past-Data-information-data-model-data-Symbolic-energetic-symbolic-whole body-symbolic-Data-information-data-knowledge-data-Delete-distort-delete-generalize-delete-Data-processing-data-information-data-Data-dialogue-data-knowledge-data-Reception-storage-reception-transmits-reception-Direction-question-direction-model-direction-Action-no action-action-let others take action-action-Patterns-programs-patterns and models-patterns-Intent-context-intent-content-intent-Data-information-data-feedback-data-Receive-storage-receive-transmission-receive-Transmit-receive-transmit-message-transmit-Intent-context-intent-content-intent-Symbols-letters-symbols-numbers-symbols-Music notes-senses-music notes-pictures-music notes- Sympathies-frailties-sympathies-strengths-sympathies-Hope-faith-hope-charity-hope-Shifts in programs-models-shifts-beliefs-shifts-Height-Lateral-height-Depth-heght-Space-enviornment-space-self-space-Nutrition-fitness-nutrition-hygiene-nutrtion-Body system-belief-body-integration-body

(UNITY/DEVIATING) Deny-refuse-deny-repress-deny-Unacknowledged-unavailable-unacknowledged-untrained-unacknowledged-Doubt-uncertainty-doubt-limiting beliefs-doubt-Similar-deviating-similar-randomness disorder-similiar-Action-function-action-process-action-Hopeless-helpless-hopeless-worthless-helpless-Stability-chaos-stability-randomness disorder-stability-Integration-reality-integration-data processing-integration-Fear-shame-fear-guilt-fear

(INTEGRATING) Admit-accept-admit-express-admit-Form-norm-form-fulfill-form-Success point-bifurcation point-success point-cross over point-success point-Delete-insert-delete-permutate-delete-Similar-unity-similiar-integrate-similar-Natural disorder-discontinuous disorder-natural disorder-unpredictable identity-natural disorder-Wholeness-totality-wholeness-correspondence-wholeness-Models-processes-models-beliefs-models-Integration-concepts-integretion-principles-integration-Success patterns-extend patterns-success patterns-considering anomalies-success patterns-Nature-function-nature-condition-nature-Outcome-condition-outcome-state-outcome

# ENERGY

(SIMILIARS)Mind-emotion-mind-body-mind-Identity-communicate-identity-create-identity-Father-mother-father-child-father-Natural-systems-natural-elements-natual-Conscious-subconscious-conscious-limbic-conscious-Reference-decision-reference-motivator-reference-Structure-patterns-structure-processes-structue-Space-time-space-matter-space-Past-present-past-future-past-Data-information-data-model-data-Symbolic-energetic-symbolic-whole body-symbolic-Data-information-data-knowledge-data-Delete-distort-delete-generalize-delete-Data-processing-data-information-data-Data-dialogue-data-knowledge-data-Reception-storage-reception-transmits-reception-Direction-question-direction-model-direction-Action-no action-action-let others take action-action-Patterns-programs-patterns and models-patterns-Intent-context-intent-content-intent-Data-information-data-feedback-data-Receive-storage-receive-transmission-receive-Transmit-receive-transmit-message-transmit-Intent-context-intent-content-intent-Symbols-letters-symbols-numbers-symbols-Music notes-senses-music notes-pictures-music notes- Sympathies-frailties-sympathies-strengths-sympathies-Hope-faith-hope-charity-hope-Shifts in programs-models-shifts-beliefs-shifts-Height-Lateral-height-Depth-heght-Space-enviornment-space-self-space-Nutrition-fitness-nutrition-hygiene-nutrtion-Body system-belief-body-integration-body

(UNITY/DEVIATING) Deny-refuse-deny-repress-deny-Unacknowledged-unavailable-unacknowledged-untrained-unacknowledged-Doubt-uncertainty-doubt-limiting beliefs-doubt-Similar-deviating-similar-randomness disorder-similiar-Action-function-action-process-action-

Hopeless-helpless-hopeless-worthless-helpless-Stability-chaos-stability-randomness disorder-stability-Integration-reality-integration-data processing-integration-Fear-shame-fear-guilt-fear

(INTEGRATING) Admit-accept-admit-express-admit-Form-norm-form-fulfill-form-Success point-bifurcation point-success point-cross over point-success point-Delete-insert-delete-permutate-delete-Similar-unity-similiar-integrate-similar-Natural disorder-discontinuous disorder-natural disorder-unpredictable identity-natural disorder-Wholeness-totality-wholeness-correspondence-wholeness-Models-processes-models-beliefs-models-Integration-concepts-integretion-principles-integration-Success patterns-extend patterns-success patterns-considering anomalies-success patterns-Nature-function-nature-condition-nature-Outcome-condition-outcome-state-outcome

# TASTE

(SIMILIARS)Mind-body-emotion-body-body-Identity-create-communicate-create-create-Father-child-mother-child-child-Natural-elements-systems-elements-elements-Conscious-limbic-subconscious-limbic-limbic-Reference-moivator-decision-motivator-motivator-Structure-processes-patterns-processes-processes-Space-matter-time-matter-matter-Past-future-present-future-future-Data-model-information-model-model-Symbolic-whole body-energetic-whole body-whole body-Data-knowledge-information-knowledge-knowledge-Delete-generalize-distort-generalize-generalize-Data-information-processing-information-information-Data-knowledge-dialogue-knowledge-knowledge-Reception-transmits-storage-transmits-transmits-Direction-model-question-model-model-Action-let others take action-no action-let others take action-let others take action-Patterns-models-programs-models-models-Intent-content-context-content-content-Data-feedback-information-feedback-feedback-Receive-transmission-storage-transmission-transmission-Transmit-message-receive-message-message-Intent-content-context-content-content-Symbols-nembers-letters-numbers-numbers-Musc notes-pictures-senses-pictures-pictures- Sympathies-strengths-frailties-strengths-

strengths-Hope-charity-faith-charity-charity-Shifts in programs-beliefs-models-beliefs-beliefs-Height-depth-Lateral-depth-Depth-Space-self-enviornment-self-self-Nutrition-hygiene-fitness-hygiene-hygiene-Body system-integration-belief-integration-integration-

(UNITY/DEVIATING) Deny-repress-refuse-repress-repress-Unacknowledged-untrained-unavailable-untrained-untrained-Doubt-limitig beliefs-uncertainty-limiting beliefs-limiting beliefs-Similar-randomness disorder-deviating-randomness disorder-randomness disorder-Action-process-function-process-process-Hopeless-worthless-helpless-worthless-worthless-Stability-randomness disorder-chaos-randomness disorder-randomness disorder-Integration-data processing-reality-data processing-data processing-Fear-guilt-shame-guilt-guilt-

(INTEGRATING) Admit-express-accept-express-express-Form-fulfill-norm-fulfill-fulfill-Success point-cross over point-bifurcation point-cross over point-cross over point-Delete-permutate-insert-permutate-permutate-Similar-integrate-unity-integrate-integrate-Natural disorder-unpredictable identity-discontinuous disorder-unpredictable identity-unpredictable identity- Wholeness-correspondence-totality-correspondence-correspondence-Models-beliefs-processes-beliefs-beliefs-Integration-principles-concepts-principles-principles-Success patterns-considering anomalies-extend patterns-considering anomalies-considering anomalies-Nature-condition-function-condition-condition-Outcome-state-condition-state-state-

## SMELL

(SIMILIARS)Mind-body-emotion-body-body-Identity-create-communicate-create-create-Father-child-mother-child-child-Natural-elements-systems-elements-elements-Conscious-limbic-subconscious-limbic-limbic-Reference-moivator-decision-motivator-motivator-Structure-processes-patterns-processes-processes-Space-matter-time-matter-matter-Past-future-present-future-future-Data-model-information-model-model-Symbolic-whole body-energetic-whole

body-whole body-Data-knowledge-information-knowledge-knowledge-Delete-generalize-distort-generalize-generalize-Data-information-processing-information-information-Data-knowledge-dialogue-knowledge-knowledge-Reception-transmits-storage-transmits-transmits-Direction-model-question-model-model-Action-let others take action-no action-let others take action-let others take action-Patterns-models-programs-models-models-Intent-content-context-content-content-Data-feedback-information-feedback-feedback-Receive-transmission-storage-transmission-transmission-Transmit-message-receive-message-message-Intent-content-context-content-content-Symbols-nembers-letters-numbers-
-numbers-Musc notes-pictures-senses-pictures-pictures- Sympathies-strengths-frailties-strengths-strengths-Hope-charity-faith-charity-charity-Shifts in programs-beliefs-models-beliefs-beliefs-Height-depth-Lateral-depth-Depth-Space-self-enviornment-self-self-Nutrition-hygiene-fitness-hygiene-hygiene-Body system-integration-belief-integration-integration-

(UNITY/DEVIATING) Deny-repress-refuse-repress-repress-Unacknowledged-untrained-unavailable-untrained-untrained-Doubt-limitig beliefs-uncertainty-limiting beliefs-limiting beliefs-Similar-randomness disorder-deviating-randomness disorder-randomness disorder-Action-process-function-process-process-Hopeless-worthless-helpless-worthless-worthless-Stability-randomness disorder-chaos-randomness disorder-randomness disorder-Integration-data processing-reality-data processing-data processing-Fear-guilt-shame-guilt-guilt-

(INTEGRATING) Admit-express-accept-express-express-Form-fulfill-norm-fulfill-fulfill-Success point-cross over point-bifurcation point-cross over point-cross over point-Delete-permutate-insert-permutate-permutate-Similar-integrate-unity-integrate-integrate-Natural disorder-unpredictable identity-discontinuous disorder-unpredictable identity-unpredictable identity- Wholeness-correspondence-totality-correspondence-correspondence-Models-beliefs-processes-beliefs-beliefs-Integration-principles-concepts-principles-principles-Success patterns-considering anomalies-extend patterns-considering anomalies-considering anomalies-Nature-condition-function-condition-condition-Outcome-state-condition-state-state-

# Chapter 17

# TOTALITY TRANSFORMATION THEORY

## HOLOGRAPHIC HUMAN TRANSFORMATION THEORY

Based on the way we develop Models, Processes, Beliefs (Worldviews). Through Integration, Concepts, Principles, and Models work together.

## FACTS:

- Humans are Natural Systems
- Humans are Systems
- The Human System is composed of Elements and Functions.

System Totalities are an entity or aggregation of Elements and Functions that form a Complete Whole or Totality. Wholeness principle, Oneness, Totality. Each Totality consists of 3 separate elements corresponding together as one, inter-relating, inter-dependently. First element of each totality associated with the senses of sound and sight. Second element of each totality associated with the senses of touch and energy. Third element of each totality associated with the senses of smell and taste.

Holographic Learning System

Holographic Health System

## TOTALITIES & THEIR ELEMENTS

1. TOTALITY: Whether manmade or God made any given system consists of other parts it is dependent upon to make it whole. *Integrating Totality*

1st Element: ACTION.
2nd Element: IDENTITY.
3rd Element: FUNCTION; of contents of the given totality.

2. OPEN SYSTEM: *Integrating Totality*

1st Element: ADMIT; Acknowledge, recognize the data in your environment.
2nd Element: ACCEPT; Create a dialogue of the data from the environment and theorize about this.
3rd Element: EXPRESS; Be a living role model of your theory.

3. CLOSED SYSTEM: *Deviating (Unity) Totality*

1st Element: DENY; Don't even notice the data in the environment. Ignore or lie about things to a point that you convince yourself that it isn't true.
2nd Element: REFUSE; Respond emotionally enough to let the environment know you will not tolerate its feedback or Data.
3rd Element: REPRESS; Minimize the feedback or Data in a way that expresses that you don't care about it.

4. TIME: *Similar Totality*

1st Element: PAST; Having existed or taken place in a period before the present.
2nd Present: PRESENT; Current, here, now.

3rd Element: FUTURE; Of, relating to or constituting a verb tense expressive of time yet to come.

5. CHOICE: *Similar Totality*

1st Element: TAKE ACTION; To do something about or for an experience, event or circumstance.
2nd Element: TAKE NO ACTION; To not do something about an experience, event or circumstance.
3rd Element: LET OTHERS TAKE ACTION; To not do something about or in response to another or others doing something.

6. NATURAL BEING (Higher Levels of Human System Function): *Similar Totality*

1st Element: IDENTITY/PERSONALITY; A condition or fact of relating to a particular person.
2nd Element: COMMUNICATION/INFORMATION; A process by which information is exchanged between individuals through a common system of symbols, signs, behaviors.
3rd Element: CREATION; The act of making, inventing or producing something new.

7. CHANGE: *Integrating Totality*

1st Element: DIRECTION; Guidance or supervision of action or conduct, explicit instructions.
2nd Element: QUESTION; An interrogative expression often used to test knowledge.
3rd Element: MODEL; A person whose behavior in a particular role is imitated by others.

8. NATURE: Nature is a Totality. Nature is the essence, inherent character or basic constitution of a person or thing. Inner force or the sum forces of an individual, controlling force in the universe. Nature is the forces distinguishable by fundamental or essence characteristics.

The external world in its entirety and genetically controlled qualities of an organism. Instinct. *Similar Totality*

1st Element: STRUCTURE; Arranged in a definite pattern or organization, an arrangement of particles or parts in a substance or body. Structure is organized parts as dominated by the general character of a whole system. Structure is the configuration, design and architecture of a whole.
2nd Element: PATTERN; Pattern is the natural or man-made configuration of a system with reliable samples of traits, acts, tendencies or other observable characteristics of a system. A system discernable and coherent based on the intended interrelationships of component parts. Structural layout, arrangement, templates of the way a thing is put together, the sequencing.
3rd Element: PROCESS; Processes are progressive and advancing in a natural phenonium marked by gradual changes that lead toward a particular result. Continual, natural or biological activity or function in a series of actions or operations, conducing to an end. Integrate sensory information received so an action or response is generalized.

9. WISDOM: *Integrating Totality*

1st Element: DATA; What is heard and seen from the environment.
2nd Element: INFORMATION; Create a dialogue of the Data and create Theories about it.
3rd Element: KNOWLEDGE; Fact or condition of knowing something through experience or association with application of it.

10. TRANSFORMATION: *Integrating Totality*

1st Element: DELETE; To eliminate, remove, blot out, cut out, erase.
2nd Element: INSERT; To put in, add to, to attach, introduce to.
3rd Element: PERMUTATE (REARANGE); Major or fundamental change as in character or condition based primarily on rearrangement of existent elements.

11. SIN: *Deviating (Unity) Totality*

1st Element: GUILT; The fact of having committed a breach of conduct, violating law, or causing offense, consciously.
2nd Element: SHAME; A painful emotion caused by conscious guilt.
3rd Element: FEAR; To be afraid, expecting with alarm.

## 12. LOVE: *Similar Totality*

1st Element: FAITH; Allegiance of duty, sincerity of intentions.
2nd Element: HOPE; Cherish a desire with anticipation.
3rd Element: CHARITY; Benevolent goodwill toward or love of humanity.

## 13. FAMILY: *Similar Totality*

1st Element: FATHER; A man who has begotten a child, or legal acknowledge his.
2nd Element: MOTHER; A woman who has conceived and given birth to a child, or legal acknowledge the child hers.
3rd Element: CHILD; An unborn or recently born person.

## 14. GOD HEAD: *Integrating Totality*

1st Element: FATHER; The First person in the Godhead. The Devine creator.
2nd Element: SON; Only Begotten Son, Jesus Christ.
3rd Element: HOLY GHOST; The third person of the Trinity.

## 15. HUMAN BRAIN: *Similar Totality*

1st Element: CONSCIOUS; Perceiving, evaluating, judging and deciding with a degree of thought or observation.
2nd Element: SUBCONSCIOUS; Existing in the mind but not immediately available to conscious, mental activities just below the threshold of conscious. Processes data prior to conscious having access to it. Subjective about data.
3rd Element: LYMBIC SYSTEM; Group of sub cortical structures of the brain that are concerned with emotion and motivation. (Hypothalamus, hippocampus and amygdale).

16. LANGUAGE PROCESSING: *Similar Totality*

1st Element: SYMBOLIC; Characterized by symbols, that stand for something else. IE: numbers, resemblance, an act representing something in the subconscious mind that has been represented.
2nd Element: ENERGETIC; Operating with or marked by vigor or effect, of or relating to energy.
3rd Element: WHOLE BODY; Having all its proper parts or components, complete physical being.

17. SUCCESS: *Integrating Totality*

1st Element: FORM; The space and structure of something, Essential nature of a thing as distinguished from its matter. IE; an Idea.
2nd Element: NORM; A standard of development or achievement derived from the average or median.
3rd Element: FULLFILL; To achieve or accomplish something set out to do.

18. REALITY: The quality or state of being real as in an event, entity or state of affairs. The Totality of real things and events, actuality of existence. *Similar Totality*

1st Element: SPACE; A limited extent in one, two or three dimensions.
2nd Element: TIME; Standard of measurement between events, circumstances or conditions.
3rd Element: MATTER; The substance of which a physical object is composed. Material substance that occupies space, has mass, and is composed predominantly of atoms consisting or protons, neutrons, and electrons, that constitutes the observable universe, and that is interconvertible with energy. A material substance of a particular kind or for a particular purpose.

19. COMMUNICATE CONTINUUM: *Similar Totality*

1st Element: TRANSMIT; To send or convey from one person or place to another.

2nd Element: RECEIVE; To come into possession of. To assimilate through the mind or senses.
3rd Element: MESSAGE; A communication in writing, in speech or by signals.

20. SPACE TIME CONTINUUM: *Integrating Totality*

1st Element: EVENT; Something that happens.
2nd Element: CONDITION; Stipulation or provision upon which the fulfillment of an agreement depends, Also circumstances.
3rd Element: PROCESS; A natural phenomenon marked by gradual changes that lead toward a particular result. A continual natural or biological activity or function

21. WORLD VIEW: *Similar Totality*

1st Element: INDIVIDUAL; Being an individual or existing as an indivisible whole, intended for one person.
2nd Element: FAMILY; A group of persons of common ancestry.
3rd Element: SOCIETY; A voluntary association of individuals for common ends, an organized group working together or periodically meeting because of common interests.

22. SELF VIEW: *Similar Totality*

1st Element: ME; Abstract self.
2nd Element: MYSELF; Reflective-self individual's temporary self, anticipating an old-self or a prime-self.
3rd Element: I; "One's-self" the whole of all aspects constituting the individuality of the person.

23. NATURAL MAN SELF VIEW: *Deviating (Unity) Totality*

1st Element: FRAILTY'S; The condition of being weak or delicate. Weakness in character or morals, liability to temptation. Fault due to a state of weakness. All drama begins with human frailty. ME.

2nd Element: SYMPATHIES; An affinity, association or relationship between persons on things wherein whatever affects on similarly affects the other. Mutual or parallel susceptibility or a condition brought about by it. Unity or harmony in action or effect. Inclination to think or feel alike. MYSELF.

3rd Element: STRENGTHS; The quality or state of being strong, capacity for exertion or endurance. Power to resist. Solidity. I

## 24. NATURAL MAN WORLD VIEW: *Deviating (Unity) Totality*

1st Element: UNCERTAINTY; INDIVIDUAL. Lack of sureness. Unsure knowledge. Not reliable. Imperfect or unknown information. Not fully confident. Lack of knowing or faith. Sureness.

2nd Element: DOUBT; FAMILY. Not accepting. A feeling of uncertainty or lack of conviction. To call into question of truth. A lack of confidence in, a distrust. Hesitate to believe. Ability

3rd Element: LIMITING BELIEFS; SOCIETY. Restrictive conviction of the truth of some statement or the reality of some phenomenon. Functioning as a limit, restrictive limiting value, being an environmental factor. Boundaries based upon programming and life's experiences. Boundless.

## 25. MEMORY: *Similar Totality*

1st Element: REAL; Relating to everyday concerns and activities: Seriously, Genuine.

2nd Element: VICARIOUS; Even that have been deleted: Imaginative or subjective response in experiences of another: Occurring, unexpected or abnormal: Another's experience of it.

3rd Element: GENETIC; Relating to and determined by the origin. Present at birth or development in childhood without needing any instruction. Ancestral, inherited, instinctual or natural.

## 26. HUMAN: *Similar Totality*

1st Element: MIND; The element or complex of elements in an individual that feels, perceives, thinks, will, reason.

2nd Element: EMOTION; The affective aspect of consciousness, feeling.
3rd Element: BODY; Organized physical substance of a being.

27. ENTROPY: *Deviating (Unity) Totality*

1st Element: DISORDER.
2nd Element: UNCERTAINTY.
3rd Element: PLUMMET.

28. META PROGRAMS: *Similar Totality*

1st Element: DATA PROCESSING; Environmental input IE: Sound, Sight.
2nd Element: INFORMATION PATTERN AND STORAGE; Dialogue of the data, identifying repetitions of dialogue filing the information in the subconscious.
3rd Element: COMPRESSING FOR MODEL MAKING; Programs in the subconscious to help file and store environmental and conscious response data into more generalized programs.

29. EDUCATE: Unique qualities, talents of each. *Integrating Totality*

1st Element: A SENSE OF COMMONALITY; Association of information with individual experience of self or others.
2nd Element: A BELONGING AND HARMONIZING OF UNIQUE INDIVIDUALITY WITH A SENSE OF COMMONALITY.
3rd Element: TO DRAW OUT.

30. CORRESPONDENCE: *Integrating Totality*

1st Element: SIMILARITIES; Associated with things in common.
2nd Element: UNITY (DEVIATIONS); All things not associated in similarities consist of deviations and must find a way of associating more similar to Unify. All things must unify to be around each other.
3rd Element: INTEGRATION; The only way deviating traits, events, education, data, conditions, anything deviating can come into unity is to Integrate. Integrating is a process of changing something of an identity

level change to get the things to integrate. To integrate is to find a common purpose of the whole from all aspects.

31. MESSAGE: *Similar Totality*

1st Element: INTENT; The state of mind in which a thing is done.
2nd Element: CONTENT; Something contained in something.
3rd Element: CONTEXT; The interrelated conditions in which something exists or occurs.

32. DATA PROCESSING: *Similar Totality*

1st Element: RECEPTION, INTERNAL PROCESSING: The act or action or instance of receiving.
2nd Element: STORAGE (MODELS AND MEMORIES): Space or place for storing; the act of storing.
3rd Element: TRANSMISSION (MODELS AND MEMORIES), TRANSMITTED THROUGH OUR LANGUAGE: To send or convey from one person or place to another. To cause or allow to spread.

33. TRANSFOMATIVE CHANGE: *Integrating Totality*

1st Element: KNOW THY SELF:
2nd Element: HEAL THY SELF:
3rd Element: KNOW AND HEAL OTHERS:

34. UNCERTAINTY: *Deviating (Unity) Totality*

1st Element: SKEPTICISM; Doctrine that true knowledge in a particular area is uncertain.
2nd Element: DOUBT; To lack confidence.
3rd Element: MISTRUST; To doubt the trust, validity or effectiveness.

35. DISORDER (UNAVAILABLE ENERGY): *Deviating (Unity) Totality*

1st Element: UNACKNOWLEDGED; Rejecting even recognizing to admit.

2nd Element: UNTRAINED; A series of parts or elements that work together to constitute a system for producing results which haven't learned the process yet.

3rd Element: UNSKILLED; Not having acquired mastery of or skill in something. (as in a technique).

36. HEALING: *Integrating Totality*

1st Element: SPIRITUAL; Ecclesiastical rather than lay or temporal.

2nd Element: ENERGY; A fundamental entity of nature that is transferred between parts of a system in the production of physical change within the system and usual regarded as the capacity for doing work.

3rd Element: PHYSICAL; Having material existence, perception through the senses and subject to the laws of nature.

37. BLOCKS: Blocks are blocked senses and the programs that are created by a combination of the sensory experience itself AND our conscious response to the sensory experience. Depending on the firing order and the sense that is blocked, you have less to zero access to every function and process in your firing pattern. You might have only half of your reference, decision or motivation ability and half of your world or self-view. *Deviating (Unity) Totality*

1st Element: MINOR; Nuero-firing order where the data if blocked but the CNS can fire through that area of the brain, but the next sense fired processes it's data and the data from the Minor blocked data.

2nd Element: MAJOR; A block in the brain of data that the CNS can not fire through and the CNS will have to backfire, back through the data it just fired through.

3rd Element: COMPLEX; Block of the data the CNS can not fire through and doesn't backfire but instead crosses over the opposite side of the body to the sensory data across from it. No other sensory data between the blocked data and the cross over data gets processed.

38. EVENT: *Integrating Totality*

1st Element: STATE; Condition of mind or temperament.

2nd Element: CONDITION; Something essential to appearance and occurrence.
3rd Element: OUTCOME; Result or consequence.

39. TOTALITY (WHOLENESS): Necessary data for conclusion of things, to determine outcome of a process. One of the individual entries in a mathematical matrix or determinant. *Integrating Totality*

1st Element: MENTAL WITH THE SENSES OF SOUND AND SIGHT.
2nd Element: EMOTIONAL WITH THE SENSES OF TOUCH AND ENERGY.
3rd Element: PHYSICAL WITH THE SENSES OF TASTE AND SMELL.

40. MAN WORLD VIEW: *Integrating Totality*

1st Element: SURENESS.
2nd Element: ABILITY.
3rd Element: BOUNDLESS.

41. MAN SELF VIEW: *Integrating Totality*

1st Element: ABILITY/STRENGTH.
2nd Element: EMPATHY.
3rd Element: STAMINA.

42. DISORDER: *Deviating (Unity) Totality*

1st Element: SIMILAR; Having characteristics in common, alike in substance or essentials.
2nd Element: DEVIATING DISORDER; Disturbing normal functions abnormally or unusually.
3rd Element: RANDOMNESS DISORDER; To disturb the regular or normal functions haphazardly.

43. ROCK BOTTOM: *Deviating (Unity) Totality*

1st Element: HELPLESS; Lacking protection or support.
2nd Element: HOPELESS; Incapable of redemption or improvement.
3rd Element: WORTHLESS; Useless.

## 44. ANOMALY: *Deviating (Unity) Totality*

1st Element: SIMILAR; Strictly comparable, having characteristics in common.
2nd Element: DEVIATING; To cause to turn from a previous course.
3rd Element: DISORDER; Disturb the regular or normal functions of.

## 45. FAR FROM EQUILIBRIUM: *Deviating (Unity) Totality*

1st Element: STABILITY; Quality or state of being stable. Not moving forward nor changing.
2nd Element: CHAOS; Confused unorganized state of primordial matter before the creation
3rd Element: RANDOMNESS DISORDER.

## 46. SENSORY INDICATORS: *Similar Totality*

1st Element: REFERENCE; Referring or consulting.
2nd Element: DECISION; A determination arrived at after consideration.
3rd Element: MOTIVATOR; Excite, energize, activate.

## 47. MAJOR DATA COMPRESSION: *Similar Totality*

1st Element: DELETE; Erase, Eliminate.
2nd Element: DISTORT; Twist out of proportion.
3rd Element: GENERALIZE; Spread or extend

## 48. DATA COMPRESSION MODELS: *Similar Totality*

1st Element: PATTERNS; A form or model proposed for imitation.
2nd Element: PROGRAMS; A plan or system under which action may be taken toward a goal.
3rd Element: MODELS; An example for imitation or emulation.

49. DIMENSION: *Similar Totality*

1st Element: HEIGHT; The extent of elevation above a level and the distance from the bottom to the top of something.
2nd Element: DEPTH; The perpendicular measurement downward from a surface, the direct linear measurement from front to back.
3rd Element: LATERAL; Extending from side to side.

50. EXPAND: *Integrating Totality*

1st Element: SPACE; A limited extent in one, two or three dimensions.
2nd Element: ENVIRONMENT; Circumstances, objects or conditions by which one is surrounded.
3rd Element: SELF; The entire person of an individual, the realization or embodiment of an abstraction.

51. PHYSICAL HEALTH MATRIX: *Integrating Totality*

1st Element: NUTRITION; The act or process of nourishing or being nourished.
2nd Element: FITNESS; The quality or state of being fit.
3rd Element: HYGIENE; Conditions or practices of cleanliness conducive to health.

52. SYSTEMS SPIRITUAL MATRIX: *Integrating Totality*

1st Element: BODY; The organized physical substance of a living or dead animal, plant or human.
2nd Element: BELIEF; A state or habit of mind in which trust or confidence is placed in some person or thing.
3rd Element: INTEGRATION; Incorporation as equals into society or an organization of individuals or different groups.

53. NOTES: *Similar Totality*

1ˢᵗ Element: MUSIC; The science or art of ordering tones or sounds in succession, in combination, and in temporal relationships to produce a composition having unity and continuity.
2ⁿᵈ Element: SENSES; The faculty of perceiving by means of sense organs. A specialized function or mechanism as sight, hearing, smell, taste, touch, by which animals, humans receive and respond to external or internal stimuli.
3ʳᵈ Element: PICTURES; A design or representation made by various means, painting, drawing, photography.

## 54. LANGUAGE: *Similar Totality*

1ˢᵗ Element: SYMBOLS; Something that stands for or suggests something else by reason of relationship, association, convention, or accidental resemblance.
2ⁿᵈ Element: LETTERS; A symbol usually written or printed representing a speech sound and constituting a unit of an alphabet.
3ʳᵈ Element: NUMBERS; A sum of units. The characteristic of an individual by which it is treated as a unit or of a collection by which it is treated in terms of units.

## 55. DATA: *Similar Totality*

1ˢᵗ Element: LITERAL.
2ⁿᵈ Element: FIGURATIVE.
3ʳᵈ Element: SYMBOLIC.

## 56. TRANSITION POINTS: *Integrating Totality*

1ˢᵗ Element: SUCCESS POINT; End of Forming Phase, fulfilled purpose.
2ⁿᵈ Element: BIFURCATION POINT; End of Norming Phase, Anomalies appear. The beginning of The Transformation Curve. (In search of New Answers).
3ʳᵈ Element: CROSS OVER POINT; A new Success Pattern will suddenly appear, (Discontinuity). Jumping the Curve, the Change Curve. Success.

## 57. THE AGE ERA OF INTEGRITY/ERA OF LIGHT: *Integrating Totality*

1st Element: UNIQUE QUALITIES, TALENTS OF EACH.
2nd Element: A SENSE OF COMMONALITY BETWEEN THE INDIVIDUAL AND THEIR ENVIRONMENT, THE COMMON THREAD THEY HAVE WITH EACH OTHER AND A BOND WITH THE NATURAL WORLD.
3rd Element: A BALANCING AND HARMANIZING OF UNIQUE INDIVIDUALITY WITH A SENSE OF COMMONALITY.

## 58. INTEGRATE: *Integrating Totality*

1st Element: DECIDE.
2nd Element: BELIEVE.
3rd Element: CHOICE.

## 59. CHI (KI): *Integrating Totality*

1st Element: BODY SYSTEMS MATRIX; Sight and Sound.
2nd Element: BELIEF INTEGRATION; Energy and Touch
3rd Element: ADDICTIVE SYSTEMS; Smell and Taste

## 60. DISCONTINUOUS DISORDER: *Integrating Totality*

1st Element: ACKNKOWLEDGE.
2nd Element: SKILL.
3rd Element: TRAIN.

## 61. PRIDE: *Deviating (Unity) Totality*

1st Element: OPINION.
2nd Element: DELIGHT.
3rd Element: SELF RESPECT.

## 62. AGENCY: *Integrating Totality*

1st Element: AGENT.
2nd Element: OPERATION.
3rd Element: INSTRUMENT.

63. PURPOSE: *Integrating Totality*

1st Element: INTENT.
2nd Element: RESOLVE.
3rd Element: EXIST.

64. FUNCTION: *Integrating Totality*

1st Element: CHARACTERISTICS.
2nd Element: NATURAL.
3rd Element: PERFORMANCE.

65. NATURE OF FUNCTION: *Integrating Totality*

1st Element: INSTRUCTION.
2nd Element: PROGRAMMING.
3rd Element: OPERATION.

66. INCREMENTAL CHANGE: *Similar Totality*

1st Element: Success patterns exploring possibilities for patterns or systems for change. Exploring to find patterns for success.
2nd Element: Extend and improve the patterns and systems for the change. Repeat the pattern over and over again.
3rd Element: The system reached its potential and also shows its built-in problems and is not open to new information, data and feedback.

67. IDENTITY LEVEL CHANGE: *Integrating Totality*

1st Element: Success patterns exploring possibilities for patterns or systems for change.

2nd Element: Extend and improve the patterns and systems for change. This is usually a process of repetition of the success patterns or systems for change.

3rd Element: Success patterns considering anomalies (problems built into the system of success from the start. Taking in new information, data and feedback for change). This is where the original success patterns or systems are taking into anomalies now apparent from the first step of change patterns. Be open to feedback new data, new information and knowledge. Address anomalies, (problems) create new success pattern which addresses the anomalies and go to Step 2 again. Repeat, repeat, repeat, pattern.

## HH MAP CORRESPONDENCE

Mental; DIRECTION

Elements

    a. Identity
    b. Data'
    c. Structure
    d. Forming
    e. Admit
    f. Perceive
    g. Data processing
    h. Transmit
    i. Intent
    j. Delete

"Concepts"; (with Principles and Models), "Integration" of Unity for inherent senses of Right and Wrong.

"Integrate" "Integrity", "Structure", unified with Interrelated "Elements".

"Structure" "Similarity" "Correspondence" insert with "Processes" of Characteristics, add to or insert.

"Structure" and "Processes" unite based upon "Similarities".

"Unity of Deviating Structure takes action, event, conditions and process.

Emotional; QUESTIONING

Integrate "Integrity"

"Patterns" to Interrelated "Elements"

"Relationships" of "Elements" to its "Content"

"Principles" already "Interrelated" and "Interdependent"

Elements:

1. Communication, information processing and storage
2. Information, dialogue, new theories with patterns
3. Processes
4. Norm
5. Accept
6. Storage
7. Information process and storage
8. Receive
9. Context
10. Insert

PHYSICAL HH MAP CORRESPONDENCE

Physical; MODELING

"Correspondence" governs Function (Purpose and Origin)

"Permutation" Character or Condition rearranges existing "Elements"

Assign an Element of 1 set to Each Element of the same or another set ("Contents").

Function governing do this based upon "Similar" "Elements"

"Similarities"; "Process".

"Integration" of "Process" of related "Elements".

"Deviating" "Processes" take an event, condition and process to "Structure".

Elements:

    a. Transmit Model through language and behaviors.
    b. Know application
    c. Patterns
    d. Fulfilled
    e. Express
    f. Transmit
    g. Compress for models
    h. Message
    i. Content
    j. Permutation

## MEMORY

Real; Relating to every day concerns and activities: Seriously, Genuine.

Vicarious; Even that have been deleted: Imaginative or subjective response in experiences of another: Occurring, unexpected or abnormal: Another's experience of it.

Genetic; Relating to and determined by the origin. Present at birth or development in childhood without needing any instruction. Ancestral, inherited, instinctual or natural.

## CLOSED SYSTEM

Deny; Not listen nor look at feedback

Refuse; Emotional response about feedback

Repress; Just brush it off some way

## OPEN SYSTEM

Admit; Listen and look at the feedback.

Accept; Consider points of value for self in the feedback.

Express; Implement through behavior any value you find for you.

WISDOM: The discerning use of knowledge, which body of knowledge is best to use where, when. Being wise means you have an elevated understanding of the entire system.

Data; Symbols themselves, letters, numbers, sensory symbols such as sounds, textures, temperature, sweet, bitter,

Information; Arrangement of data into meaningful patterns (such as math, physics)

Knowledge; The application and productive use of information. Knowledge is built on the models we form out of experience and theories.

## DATA PROCESSING

Reception; A complete acknowledgment of all data.

Storage; Subconscious processing data along with conscious awareness and input.

Transmit; Express to the environment the conscious awareness.

## META PROGRAMS

Data Processing; Major and Minor Data compression programs. Information and Patterns.

Storage; Neuron firings and programs and models already created subconsciously and creating new programs and models.

Compressing for Model making; Symbolizing the programs and models for quick and easy access by conscious.

SUCCESS

Form; Explore possibilities until success patterns are discovered or invented.

Norm; The success patterns are repeated over and over.

Fulfill; Success begins to flatten a bit still rising, growth is now achieved by integrating differences and modifications into the original pattern at this the system reaches its peak then begins to decline, having attained its fullest possibilities of expression.

EDUCATE: Unique qualities, talents of each.

A sense of commonality between the individual and their environment, the common thread they have with each other and a bond with the natural world.

A belonging and harmonizing of unique individuality with a sense of commonality.

To Draw Out.

WORLDVIEW

Individual; Self view

Family; DNA overlays of parents and sibling patterns on the self

Society; Culture beliefs and issues

SIN

Guilt; Behavioral expressions as a result of disowning one's potential.

Shame; Inner emotional response due to the inner knowing of the true self.

Fear; Not recognizing one's own abilities and strengths.

## PURE LOVE OF CHRIST

Hope; One's thoughts for better

Faith; Emotions felt in response to and supporting these thoughts

Charity; Behaviors expressing belief of one's character and knowledge relating to these

## REALITY

The quality or state of being real, the totality of real things and events.

Space; A period of time, also it's duration a limited extent in 1, 2, or 3 dimensions: A boundless 3-dimensional extent in which objects and events occur and have relative position and direction, beyond earth's atmosphere and solar system.

Time; A measurable period during which an action process or condition exists or continues: Non-spatial continuum that is measured in terms of events which exceed one another from past through present to future.

Matter; Physical material substance actually occupying space, composed of atoms, consisting of protons, neutrons and electrons, that constitutes the observable universe and is interconvertible with energy

## TIME

Past: Mental processes.

Present: Emotions.

Future: Behaviors and Models.

FAMILY

Father; A man who has begotten children.

Mother; A woman who has borne children.

Child; An unborn or recently born human being.

COMMUNICATION

Transmit; Send out one's thoughts.

Receive; Be consciously aware in the present of what is sent.

Message; The underlying theme or meaning.

MESSAGE

Intent; The design or purpose of.

Content; The principle substance offered.

Context; Interrelated conditions in which something exists or occurs.

DIMENSION

Height; Distance from bottom to top.

Lateral; Extending from side to side.

Depth; Direct linear measurement from front to back.

Consciousness is a shape given form by space and dimension.

Thoughts are things: the intellectual product or the organized views of our beliefs: An individual's actions are the product of thought. Movement has meaning. Where and How you move gives meaning to movements. The more Tactile you are the more you treat ideas as things.

The less tactile you are the less you treat ideas as things. i.e.: "Oh my God" hand to eye or forehead= emotional. Arm raised in air= physical.

# TOTALITY TECHNIQUE

Determine from the list of TOTALITIES, the specific 1 you will use for doing this technique. Write on 3 separate pieces of paper the Functions of the Totality and place them on the ground in their order of 1, 2 and 3. They are listed in their proper order on the page listing the Totalities. Make sure to have space between each piece of paper to take one or two steps as you will walk from one to the other through this technique.

Stand, with space for 2 steps between yourself and the first Function on the ground.

"Now, imagine or pretend to imagine, placing your entire life's experiences between yourself and the first positioned Function on the ground." (pause and watch them, giving them time to place this on the ground).

"Not, now, but in a moment, I'll instruct you to walk through your life's experiences and stand on the first Function placed on the ground, in front of you. When you arrive at the first Function you will stand there, with your eyes opened or closed, that's entirely up to you. I will guide you through the Function process for this first Function regarding your life's experience. Thank you, please walk through your life's experience now and stop on the first Function."

(Pause and give them a moment to do this).

"Not now, but in a moment, I will guide you through this first Function processes. These are Filters in the subconscious and this first filter is Perception, Identity and Personality. These are of your Past and you may now choose of yourself the Data from your life's experience for you to use to expand upon for your Personality, your Identity, of your choosing. The symbols, dates, sounds, sights, intuitions, textures, smells and tastes and energies. All of these in simple or complex symbols of your choosing, and placing these symbols into a internal structures of character traits, mental and emotional traits. Expanding and joining any symbols and representations of a similar basis. Taking symbols and all this Data, of your choosing and noticing any symbols of this for you which might deviate from the other symbols and imagine or pretend to imagine adjusting the Different symbols so they become more similar with each other, more similar with the collection of symbols as you have chosen. These to be your filter of your Perception, for your Identity, for your Personality, as you choose to be. " (Focus your instructions including the Totality Functions they have laid on the ground into your dialogue of instructions to them as you guide them through each step in your dialogue.) (Pause and allow them some time to complete this process, you might repeat some of the instruction over to assist them in completing this first step.) (When they have completed this step be sure to thank them. Then continue with the technique instructions.)

"Now, please, taking all of the collection of symbols and senses and Data you have chosen for your Identity, Personality and Perceptions regarding all of your life's experience, imagine or pretend to imagine placing all of these on the ground in front of you, between yourself and the second Filter you have placed upon the ground. And after you have done this again, walking through all of this Data from your life's experience, walk through all of this and stand upon the second Filter placed upon the ground, in front of you." (Pause, giving them time to complete this process. Again, you may repeat the instructions and pause, giving them time to complete this. When they have done this and have walked through their life's experience and are standing on the second filter, continue with the dialogued instructions.)

"Thank you. Now, this Data you choose imagine, or pretend to imagine making models and different patterns of this Data and symbols. Create your own sentences, dialogues, information about these symbols and the

Data. Unify and Integrate the Data into dialogue, sentences for internal information for you, they may naturally become dialogue and sentences and information, some might require your assistance in relating to some of the other models and patterns and you may imagine or pretend to imagine multiplying some with common symbols and dialogues of your choosing for you purpose for your life's experience. Noticing any deviations or anomalies and integrating these with common multiples to create your sentences, your dialogue for your information. For your internal processing for your present moments for your experiences. From your dialogue and sentences of the Data create New Theories for your life's experience. New applications and productive use for you personally from the information. Creating meaningful patterns to use in each moment of your life, built upon your Life's New Theories, new applications for you to experience. Create communication patterns for these New theories and models, so they may interact and relate with one another and be in correspondence with your New Theories for your life's New experiences.

Rearranging any information you choose to in order to create any New Theories you may choose to create for your life's experiences." (Add in any other aspects pertaining to the specific Filtering process they have chosen and are standing on, dialogue this also into your instructions and guiding them.)

(You may read the guidelines through again as they take some time to process this part of the technique. Give them plenty of time to do so and repeat the guidelines to assist them. Pause and read until they indicate that they have completed these instructions. Remember, they can either imagine doing the process or even just pretend to imagine doing the process.)

(When they have completed this part of the technique, thank them and continue to the third part of this technique.) And Information from the experiencing of your New Theories (add in here also any specific dialogue pertaining to the specific Functions for Totalities they have chosen and are walking through). On the ground, in front of you, between yourself and the third filter. (Give them time to do this or to imagine doing this or to pretend to imagine doing this. You might repeat the instructions to assist them with this process. When you know they have completed this, continue with the technique.)

"Thank you, Now, if you may, please, with all of your life's experiences, filtering to your choosing, continuing, of your, choosing, gather Knowledge, Discerning, Understandings, for your Life's Completeness. Of your choosing, Create or imagine to Create Models, Beliefs, as you choose and for you to use, to share with yourself, with others in your life, for Your Wholeness of Life. Create or imagine or pretend to imagine to Create your Language processes, your Behaviors, the way you Express and Expand you, as a Whole, Entire Being, of your choosing. Process the Data, Information, Dialogues, New Theories, Experiences and Applications and you Choose or imagine or pretend to imagine your Knowledge from all this. You choose or imagine to choose, your Discernments of all this. You may Expand on Similarities and adjust Differences, you may Add to or Delete from, of your choosing, for your processes of Being and Expressing of your Wholeness. Your words, their placement in you Expressions, your Doings, for your Expressions, the Whole Representation of the Totality of you and your life's experience, Choosing the Knowledge gained, choosing the ability to Discern, to Create your Whole life, according to your choosing as you imagine or pretend to imagine it to be, of your choice.. Each aspect from the Data and Structure through the Information and the Patterns, the Knowledge and Discernments with the Processes, all Open to one another, matching Similar with one another, adjusting any Deviations or Anomalies with one another and becoming more One, Whole, Unified, in a common Purpose, Expression, Creating, ongoing throughout your Whole life's Experience and Expressing. All that you may imagine or pretend to imagine, you may Create and be One within yourself, in charge of your life's Experience. Continually Creating New Life's Models, open to the Information and Theories, newly on going and Data and Experiences and Creating Processes and Models for continual New Expressions in a literal sense and new Creations in your life." (Give them time to process this part of the technique you may read this until they have completed the instructions. Add in any other specific instructions pertaining to the specific Function they have placed on the ground.)

(When they have completed this part of the technique, Thank them and have them step off the last Function Filter and go to where they began and walk straight through the beginning point to the last Filter, get off again, go to the beginning point and walk to the end again and again until you notice a subconscious shift in them.)

# Chapter 18

# BEING LEADS TO HAVING

We are limitless beings. By just using 10% of our brain, we will be genius. The subconscious part of our brain mass will never be able to be exactly duplicated by man. Our conscious thought waves are more powerful than Wi-Fi. The chemical codes of our emotions encode their imprints through our thought waves onto others. We are true, pure energy and as such, will never cease to exist. It is entirely our choice as to what it is that we become, we are not limited by any potential lack. We are only limited by our own self- limiting beliefs.nMan has been partial to his own wisdoms and knowledge since we began life on earth. We are still dependent upon other people's knowledge to guide us. The potential of the human brain is limitless.

Our materialistic, capitalist culture engenders, promotes, and supports an Identity that essentially lacks; known as "The Wanna' Self." This is done by its worship of results, its career and job orientation, and its insatiable demand for productivity. Most of America still embraces the Protestant Work Ethic and so have tacitly agreed to the following formula:

*DOING LEADS TO BEING LEADS TO HAVING:*

Performing or executing actions guides the way and corrects the course for the function of our quality and state of having an existence which guides the way and corrects the course of our maintaining possessions, privilege and entitlements.

This Outside-In Approach to life has indeed brought about lots of satisfaction, success, and prosperity, but is no longer adequate as a success model today.

This Industrial Age formula has been replaced by the Information Age Formula:

*BEING LEADS TO DOING LEADS TO HAVING:*

The quality or state of having an existence executes action and guides the way correcting the course, performing and executing actions that guides the way correcting the course for function to maintain our possessions, privileges and entitlements.

This is an Inside-Out Approach and yet it is not enough, since it still makes a separation between the Inside and Outside. What is needed is an Integrated Approach that not only links the Inner World with the Outer World, but can describe the intimate connections between the two. This is a Whole System Approach, its formula is:

*BEING LEADS TO HAVING:*

The quality or state of existence guides the way, correcting the course as the function to indicate movement or action thereby maintaining possessions, privilege and entitlement.

Notice that Doing is missing. The logical question would be: Who will do what needs to be done? A world cannot function without action; without some part of the system doing something. Stillness, it would seem, results in Nothingness.

To understand this apparently impossible approach, it is important to look at the following two premises:

*PREMISE #1: YOU ARE THE UNIVERSE*

*PREMISE #2: THE UNIVERSE IS MADE FOR YOUR SUCCESS*

If there is no separation between you and the universe, and it truly is an extension of you and your consciousness, and if it is designed for your success; then just like your thought can make your hands pick up a glass of water, the universe can move in such a way that your dreams and desires are met. In other words, the universe rearranges itself to accommodate your picture of reality. To be more accurate, it would be better to say your "model" of reality.

So, shifting your fundamental model of reality, your world view, results in a shift; a corresponding set of actions by the universe. A flower does very little, it releases a sweet smell that brings the action-oriented bees. Notice that leaders do very little manual labor compared to those who do the hard work in an organization. Traditionally their tasks are more mental, and more recently many experts believe that they have become more spiritual in nature. What type of world-view brings about these spiritual visions of a compelling future? With which of these three levels do you identify with the most?

The Metaphysical Foundation involving substance and active forces. Universal gravitation (rather than conservation of.) Reality beyond what is perceivable by the human senses (Philosophy).

Impressed Force – Force is not an internal property of a single body by which that body determines the (temporal) evolution of its own future state. Force is an action of one body on another essentially distinct by which the first body change is the state of the second body. Fare from expanding the state of motion of a single body, force has nothing at all to do with the state of motion of the body that exerts it. Force expresses a relationship of Real Interaction between two bodies which one body changes the state of motion of the other.

Newton's third law: The equality of action and reaction. Every change of the quality of motion of body is counter balanced by corresponding change in the quantity of change motion of a second body where the first body is the cause of the change of motion of the second body and Visa Versa the third law expresses a (dynamical) community or real interaction of material (substances), (Momentum, or mass multiplied by velocity). A property of a moving body that the body has by virtue of its mass and motion and that is equal to the product of the body's mass and velocity: A property of a moving body that determines the length of time required to bring it to rest when under the action of a constant force of moment. Strength or force gained by motion or through the development of events. It will build up speed that will tend to maintain itself. Giving meaning to motion itself. (True motions) in a system of interacting (corresponding) bodies are as the center of mass frame of the system which make the third law true. Active or functioning state or condition. An impulse or inclination of the mind or will. Velocity is the rate of change of position along a straight line with respect to time: the derivative of position with respect to time. Rate of occurrence and action, historical change.

The significance of the concept of mass is simple to solve by a definition of the concept of true for absolute motion. Apply the law of motion to the observed. Laws of Motion are ultimately grounded in a priori of conditions of possibilities of experience. These facts describe the priori conditions that make objective empirical thinking possible in the first place (Having unknown short distances between with definite forces running into infinity), (May appear as opaque constants, hard to explain and understand, invariable and unchanging as of a fixed value in a given situation or universally or that is characteristic of some substance or instrument, a term of logic with a fixed designation).

----------------------------------------------------------------------Open and Closed Systems; basically, we are not open systems anymore. We are closed systems, and our boundaries are not permutable therefore we have no ability to exert any force of our being for success. As closed systems we are imprisoned in our own self-limiting beliefs and will just keep repeating our same failures.

Unbridge-ability is about choices, choice is a quantum leap syndrome. There is an abrupt change, sudden increase, or dramatic advance. An abrupt transition from one discrete energy state to another. Be willing to let go to be one with self and God and move to goals, nurture self when others are not willing to choose to go with you, they choose to stay.

Human beings are born with Quantums; 1 per each human sense:

Sound: Right - Sight: Wrong

Touch: God - Energy: Self

Taste: Life - Smell: Death

These Quantums are God-Given and never leave us here on Earth. No matter how hard we may try to numb or quiet them, they never calm down nor just go away.

We have an inner sense of all of these Quantums, and they constantly remind us of their, and our own purpose. When we accept these and listen to them, we are happy and more positive. When we try to ignore or conquer them, we struggle.

Mind, Body, and emotions (spirit) has two quantum leaps each.

Right and Wrong

God and Self

Life and Death

Choice of the first three implies choice of the last three leaps. Resistance occurs when the associated Quantum changes (rest of set) is not bridgeable. When all Quantum states become bridgeable, Quantum leaps dissolve and Awareness of Unity occurs. The seventh sense: Self and Time.

Quantum leaps also applied between the third and fourth sensory firings as the details of the ways of dealing with the anomalies showing up in the third sense fired, to be able to continue with the transformative change process. The Transformative change process keeps the senses from closing and keeps Identity growing and progressing successfully.

Know Thy Self

Then Heal Thy Self

This process must happen before we can truly Know Others then Heal Others. As Jesus said we must first take the rafter out of our own eye before we can take out of another's eye.

An excellent way to truly know yourself is to know your inner self, your subconscious self. If just knowing yourself consciously only, and yet you still can't overcome or attain what your conscious knows, get to know your subconscious self and you can then consciously overcome your problems better, you can consciously attain your conscious goals. Conscious can override subconscious. First conscious must know the subconscious programs that are running.

Unbridgeability IS about choice. Unbridgeability is to be against, to be unaccepted, unabsorbed, unaccredited, unacknowledged. Choice is a quantum leap syndrome. There are 3 different aspects regarding Choice: 1) Take Action, 2) Take no Action, 3) Let another Take Action. Choice, being an option, alternative, preference, selection and or election. Be willing to let go to be self and God. Nurture self when others are not willing to choose to go with you, they choose to stay.

When the Quantum's are not bridgeable, we have Resistance in our lives: An act or instance of opposition as an ability by a very nature to go against something. A natural opposition within the system.

When the Associated Quantum's are Bridgeable we do not have Resistance in our lives.

Bridging the Quantum's take you to a point of Transformation. If bridging the Quantum's you bridge from the left side to the right side. Beginning from the top of the Map to the bottom of the Map. Corresponding Wrong with Right, Self with God and Death with Life.

Quantum leaps:

Right and Wrong

Right: Conforming with or conformable to justice, law. Continue from above. Not spurious, genuine. Just, sound, legal, proper. Toward, on the right, in a straight line and To restore to proper. Being in accordance with what is just, good, or proper. Conforming to facts or truth.

Wrong: Not on conformity with fact or truth, incorrect or erroneous. In a wrong course and Sometimes contrary to, An unjust or injurious act, To go astray or alter. Principles, practices, or conduct contrary to justice, goodness, equity or law. Not right or proper according to a code, standard or convention.

God and Self

God; The supreme or ultimate reality; the Being perfect in power, wisdom, and goodness who is worshipped as creator and ruler of the universe. A being or object believed to have more than natural attributes and powers and to require human worship, one controlling a particular aspect or part of reality.

Self; The total, essential, particular being of a person. The entire person of an individual, the realization or embodiment of an abstraction. An individual's typical character or behavior. The union of elements (as body, emotions, thoughts, and sensations) that constitute the individuality and identity of a person. Of the same character throughout, of the same material. Many words beginning with self have been added to the dictionary.

Life and Death

Life: The property or quality that distinguishes living. To continue from above. A principle or force that is considered to underlie the distinctive quality of animate beings. The sequence of physical process of living. A specific phase of earthly existence. The form or pattern of something existing in reality.

Death: The act of dying, termination of life. A permanent cessation of all vital functions. The cause or occasion of loss of life.

These synthesis with:

Sound; Right

Sight; Wrong

Touch; God

Energy; Self

Smell; Death

Taste; Life

The Quantum Leaps are a Continuum. A continuum is a coherent whole characterized as a collection, sequence, or progression of values or Elements varying by minute degrees. Good and bad stand at opposite ends of a continuum instead of describing the two halves of a line (William Shumaker). The set of real numbers include both the rationales and the irrationals: broadly; a compact set which cannot be separated into two sets neither of which contains a limit point of the other. It is continuous, marked by uninterrupted extension in space, time or sequence. Of a Function: having the property that the absolute value of the numerical difference between the value at a given point and the value at any point on a neighborhood of the given point can be made as close to zero as desired by choosing the neighborhood small enough, continuum (To continue to hold together).

There must needs be opposition in all things and the Quantum Leaps are opposites; Right/Wrong, God/Self, Life/Death. Each of the Abstract or

Conscious Functions apply to each Quantum relating to its position on the Holographic Human Map as well as the sense it is with. There can be no Right without Wrong nor Wrong without Right. There can be no God without Self nor Self without God. There is no Life without Death or Death without Life. I have heard it said that in a "Sense", there is no Right or Wrong, there is no God or Self, there is no life or death. Pick and choose for yourself, but don't let the interpretations of man lead you astray. It is also stated in scriptures that Lucifer will tell you 99 truths to get you to believe 1 lie.

Bridging the Quantum consists of being open to the Wrong within Right and the Right within the Wrong. The God within Self and the Self within God, as well as the Life within Death and the Death within Life. Just as the story of the Garden of Eden in the Bible, when the Lord placed Adam and Eve there to multiply and replenish the Earth and placed a Tree of Knowledge of Good and Evil but commanded them to not eat of its fruit. The short version here, is the fact that had they kept the Lord's commandment and not ate of the "Apple tree", they would not have even known they were naked.

There is always a Transition or Crossover point. Always a quantum bridging between historic change; something must come to an end for something completely different to come into existence.

We have mentioned prior of a $7^{th}$ Sense, a sense of Self and God and/or a sense of Time. This $7^{th}$ sense has the Primary Question "When?" As with the other Quantum's, this sense also represents the other Abstract and conscious, Subconscious Functions already a part of this on the Holographic Human Map. This $7^{th}$ sense, as relating to the Quantum Leap represents the Great I Am and the Eternal Now.

MENTAL: Past, Intent, Identity, time, thoughts in the form of images and sounds and internal dialogues.

- ➤ Sound: Deletes by comparison/matching. Sound information deleted by the subconscious is not discarded. The subconscious deletes the information that doesn't fit based on the individual's current mind state. Deleted information is kept in holding until it has enough information from conscious to create a new generalization. Detailed oriented, asks and knows "what"? values, ethics ideals honoring self. Sound and its processes are subjective; the dictionary defines subjective as proceeding from or taking place in a human's mind rather than the external world, personal subjective. Quantum Leap Is Right, Intent.

> Sight: Deletes by contrast, (again: deleted information is not destroyed, it is kept in holding until conscious give subconscious enough information to make a new generalization. scope oriented, ideas, reasons, concepts. Quantum Leap Is Wrong, Intent. Sight is objective defined as of or having to do with an object external, not influenced by emotions or personal prejudices. When one is missing a sense from the mental processing they will come across and have a shallow concept of things.

EMOTION: Present, context, distort, communication, positive and negative emotions.

> Touch: towards, distorts by amplification, distortion is done to make a subtitle of the generalization. Present, knows and asks "who?. Touch is subjective. Quantum Leap Is God, Context, Space. Intuition: Actions, present, asks and knows "which"? distorts by diminishing, context, space. Relationships and the way things relate.
> Energy: Intuitions -Energy is objective. Quantum Leap Is Self. When one is missing information from one of these senses they will have a constricted use or application of things. Intuitions, actions, distortions by diminishing to make generalizations.

BODY: Future, content, generalize.

> Taste: beliefs about character, skill, competence, capability. Qualities of being, generalized by sameness, chops off other parts to generalize, asks and knows "how"? Quantum Leap Is Life, content. Matter body, physical. -Taste is subjective.
> Smell: Beliefs about the nature of things, the way things work, beliefs about doings and skill, asks and knows "where", generalizes by

differences, quantum leap is death, content, matter, body, physical. Smell is objective. When one is missing information from one of these senses they will have a narrow structure of things.

The seventh sense: The sense of self and/or time is the wholeness the totality of all the senses. It is the great I Am, the Chi. And knows and asks, "when"? This represent when the other six senses have completed their cycle successfully.

Human Beings have characteristics and attributes representative of sympathies, frailties, strengths and by nature of their minds can process and evaluate their lives and many other things.

They have a conscious existence and may perceive and conceive other things into real existence. Human, by their very nature have transformed their actions and processes not only our world but even on a DNA level of many other living things.

In order to Transform, the key of the formula affecting Transformation is FUNCTION. Function is the literal operation that converts one thing into another. Function is changed by doing any or all of the following: Deleting, Inserting, or Permutation.

Integration is a process of unifying (Unity). Humans Transform and Integrate by nature. Their inherent sense of right and wrong, in accordance with and determined by their very nature.

Permutation is major and fundamental change (as in a character or condition), based primarily on rearrangement of existent elements. Changing by the act or process, the lineal order of and ordered set or arrangements of character or conditions.

A Quantum Leap is an abrupt Transition (as of an electron, an atom, molecule) from one discrete energy state to another.

Identity and sameness of essential or genetic character in different instances. Sameness in all that constitutes the objective reality of a thing. A quality whose effect is to leave the multiplied unchanged (The number that is to be multiplied by another).

Communication being a process by which information is exchanged between individuals through a common system of symbols, signs or behaviors, exchange of information. Children reflect denied needs and repressed desires of parents and siblings.

Communication: The act or process of transferring Data.

Healing Model: 2 approaches: 1) Physical, 2): Spiritual.

1): Physical= Nutrition, Fitness, Hygiene Body Maintenance

2): Spiritual= Body System Matrix, Belief Integration, Addictive Systems (Closed), Energy System.

Language of emotions as they relate to the Holographic Human Model.

Innocence: In No Sense. Innocence breeds more Innocence.

Humiliation is the ultimate strategy of limitation.

Properties and characteristics of our natural being need not be formed or added onto, only expanded. The Inner World of Being is different than the Outer World of Doing. Human Beings are good and deserving by Nature.

Models- forming internal representations of our experiences.

A Model is not a Memory, it is a collection of Memories.

PARADIGMS (Programs in the Human Subconscious)

# Chapter 19

# BRIDGING THE QUANTUMS

BRIDGING THE QUANTUMS
Bridging is Choice (about)
Do something, Do nothing, Let others Do:
Take Action
Take No Action
Let Others Take Action

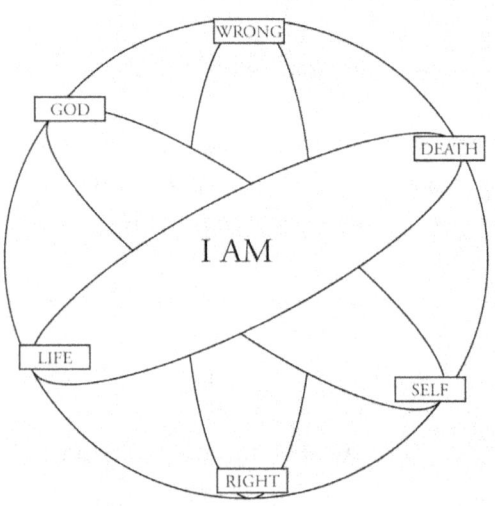

When joining the Quantum's begin on the left side and combine to the right side.

Begin at the top and go down.

Answer these questions about self not generalized or about others.

## WRONG BECOMES RIGHT

*Begin at Why (Wrong) and face What (Right): take 1 step at a time answering each question.

1. Why do you not see the truth?
2. Name your reasons of injustice or injurious?
3. Name you ideas that are contrary to your standards?
4. Why is your life incorrect or wrong?
5. What reasons or value is in this?

*Be halfway to Right (at time, when).

1. What value comes in conforming to fact?
2. What meaning is there in the injustice or injury?
3. What ethics support your ideas of restoring to proper?
4. What of your reasons and meanings are genuine?
5. What action may you take to bring value to your ideas?

*Be at Right (turn and face wrong) taking 1 step at a time to When/Time.

1. What action will you do to bring your concepts forward?
2. What action does it require see and hear the truth together?
3. Why is action required to bring reason to right?

4. Name 3 actions you may take today to bring value and meaning to their incorrect parts of your life?

*Be at When (Time). Read back you answers in a weave, then repeat:

Why is for what while what for is why. Reasons with value, ethics in concepts, 1 of many becoming 1 and the individual, the being is 1. I am that I am.

## SELF BECOMES GOD

*Go to Which (Self) walking to Who (God): Take 1 step at a time answering each questions.

1. Which is the most important of your possibilities?

2. Which behaviors may you stop to reach these?

3. Of all your intuitions, which describes the essential of your individuality?

4. With you being the first person, which functions best describe you in a group?

5. Name 3 behaviors, actions to stop to be the totality of your self?

*Be halfway to Who (at time, when).

1. Who is supreme of your possibilities?

2. Who knows the totality of you and which actions may you stop taking to become supreme?

3. Who relates best to you in your infinite mind?

4. Describe the identity of perfect in power and wisdom?

5. Name 3 actions to stop to have this?

*Be at Who (God) and face Which (Self): taking 1 step at a time to When/Time.

1. In which moment may you become your supreme?

2. Name actions you must stop to feel more than natural powers and attitudes?

3. Upon stopping these actions describe your total self in regards to being able to be creator and ruler of your own reality?

4. When your intuitions stop your actions describe your relationship with God?

*Be at When (Time). Read back your answers in a weave, then repeat:

> Which becomes who rather than individual. Which action and intuitions is the identity of supreme value. Still, the role in wisdom and total self-identity among all possibilities. I am that I am.

## DEATH BECOMES LIFE

*Go to Where (Death) walking to How (Life): take 1 step at a time answering each questions.

1. Name the situation in your life causing you ruin?

2. Describe the primary concerns or importance of things unreal, untrue or beyond endurance?

3. Name the actions others could take to address these?

4. Where is the end of all these vital functions?

5. List 3 natures of ending?

*Be half way to How (at time, when).

1. How has the sequences of your existence made your physical and spiritual experiences?

2. Describe the character traits of the patterns in your life that bring purpose and usefulness?

3. Give 3 or more aspects of the purpose of living?

4. State 3 or more questions regarding your reactions to stimuli?

5. Name states characterized by others to assist you in growth?

*Be at How (Life) and face Where (Death): taking 1 step at a time to When/Time.

1. In time how may others be a force of principles in your life?

2. In the continuum of your experiences how can your transcend your durations?

3. Name at least 3 destructive qualities of letting others take action?

4. Describe and explain the force behind questions?

5. Name characteristic of and strategies others have to assist you in purpose?

*Be at When (Time). Read back you answers in a weave, then repeat:

Situations and circumstance and a state and condition. Respect and a questions and manners of existence. Let others take action in the method still valuing the process of all. I am that I am.

-End Technique-

Algorithms based upon human senses including the Holographic Human sensory data information is associated with the sensory algorithms.

The First Element of each Totality is associated with the sense of sound and sight.

The Second Element of each Totality is associated with the sense of touch and energy.

The Third Element of each Totality is associated with the sense of taste and smell.

Based upon this association the senses of Sound and Sight are all First Elements, the sense of Touch and Energy are all Second Elements, and the sense of Taste and Smell are all Third Elements. This is the Elements used to create the Algorithms per sense for Bridging Quantum's, whether just associated Quantum's or if you are Bridging all of the Quantum's.

One Level of Elements per Sensory Reference:

The Algorithms are created based upon the Physics of Correspondence: Similar, Unity (Deviating), and Integrating, based upon the First Element of Correspondence being Similar, Second Element of Correspondence being Unity and Third Element of Correspondence being Integrate.

ALGORITHM for Sense of Sound and Sight: Similar:

Totality Sets of Totalities for first Element, second Element and third Elements per sensory reference.

First Element Totality Sets:

Similar

Family, Godhead, Closed System

Communicate, Meta Program, Data Process

Language, Message, Symbol

Blocks, Data compression, Data Compression modes

Human, Human Brain, Sensory Indicators

Memory, Change, Dimension

Whole Human, Physical Health, Spiritual Health

Time, Nature, Reality

Choice, Educate, Notes

Sin, Love, Universal Language

Second Element Totality Sets:

Unity

Disorder, Natural Man, Complete Disorder

Rock Bottom, Far from Equilibrium, Entropy

Self-view, Natural Man Self, Anomalies

Third Element Totality Sets:

Integrate

Open System, Neg-entropy, Transformation change

Space-time continuum, Event, Expand

Transformation, Correspondence, Transition Points

World View, Age of Integrity, Integrate

Physical, Spiritual, Healing

Totality, Wisdom,

Totalities put together in groups of 3's for the purpose of creating sets of 3 for Correspondence for Continuums into algorithms.

Similar Sets in 3:

1) Family, Godhead, Closed

2) Communicate, Meta Program, Data Process

3) Language, Message, Universal Language

4) Blocks, Data Compression, Data Compression Modes

5) Human, Human Brain, Sensory Indicators

6) Memory, Change, Dimension

7) Mind, Physical, Spiritual

8) Time, Nature, Reality

9) Choice, Educate, Notes

Totalities Sets of 3 for Unity Continuum:

1) Disorder, Complete Disorder, Natural Man

2) Entropy, Far From Equilibrium, Rock Bottom

3) Self view, Natural Man Self view, Anomaly

Totalities Sets of 3 for Integrate Continuum:

1) Open System, Neg-entropy, Transformation change

2) Space Time Continuum, Event, Expand

3) Transformation, Correspondence, Transition Points

4) World view, Age of Integrity, Integrate

5) Wisdom, Totality,

6) Physical, Spiritual, Healing

# CHAPTER 20

# ALGORITHM OF ELEMENTS

Sound and Sight/Similar: First Elements of different Totalities put together in sets of 3 Elements for each set, based upon Similarity of Whole Totalities and First, Second or Third Element.

SOUND AND SIGHT

Quantum's: Right and Wrong

First Elements Only.

>>>>Similar 1st Elements>>>>(A1/Family, God Head, Closed)>Father, Father-Father, Deny-Father/Father-Father, Father, Deny-Father/Father-Deny, Father-Deny, Deny/(B2/Communicate, Meta Program, Data Process)>Transmit, Data Processing-Transmit, Reception-Transmit/Transmit-Data Processing, Data Processing, Reception-Data Processing/Transmit-Reception, Data Processing-Reception, Reception/(B3/Language, Message, Universal Language)>Symbolic, Intent-Symbolic, Symbols-Symbolic/Symbolic-Intent, Intent, Symbols-Intent/Symbolic-Symbols, Intent-Symbols, Symbols/(C4/Blocks, Data Compression, Data Compression Modes)>Major, Delete-Major, Patterns-Major/Major-Delete, Delete, Patterns-Delete, Major-Patterns, Delete-Patterns, Patterns/(C5/Human, Human Brain, Sensory Indicators)>Identity, Mind-Identity, Reference-Identity/Identity-Mind, Mind, Reference-Mind/Identity-Reference, Mind-Reference, Reference/(C6/Memory, Change, Dimension)>Real, Direction-Real, Height-Real/(C7/Mind, Physical

Health, Spiritual Health)>Mind, Nutrition-Mind, Body-Mind/Mind-Nutrition, Nutrition, Body-Nutrition/Mind-Body, Nutrition-Body, Body/(D8/Time. Nature, Reality)>Past, Structure-Past, Space-Past/Past-Structure, Structure, Space-Structure, Past-Space, Structure-Space, Space/(D9/Choice, Educate, Notes)>Take action, Qualities-Take action, Music-Take action/Take Action-Qualities, Qualities, Music-Qualities/Take action-Music, Qualities-Music, Music/>>>>Unity first Elements>>>>(U10/Disorder, Complete Disorder, Natural Man)>Doubt. Similar-Doubt, Uncertainty-Doubt/Doubt-Similar, Similar-Uncertainty-Similar/Doubt-Uncertainty, Similar-Uncertainty, Uncertainty/(U11/Entropy, Far from Equilibrium, Rock Bottom)>Form, Stable-Form, Helpless-Form/Form-Stable, Stable, Helpless-Stable/Form-Helpless, Stable-Helpless, Helpless/(U12/Self-view, Natural man, Anomaly)>Me, Frailty-Me, Similar-Me/Me-Frailty, Frailty, Similar-Frailty/Me-Similar, Frailty-Similar, Similar/>>>>Integrate first Elements>>>>(I13/Open System, Neg-entropy, Transformation change)>Admit, Form-Admit, Know Thy Self-Admit/Admit-Form, Form, Know Thy Self-Form/Admit-Know Thy Self, Form-Know Thy Self, Know Thy Self/(I14/Space-time-continuum, Event, Expand)>Event, State-Event, Space-Event/Event-State, State, Space-State/Event-Space, State-Space, Space/(I15/Transform, Correspondence, Transition Points)>Delete, Unity-Delete, Success-Delete/Delete-Unity, Unity, Success-Unity/Delete-Success, Unity-Success, Success/(I16/World-view, Age-of-integrity, Integrate)>Individual, Unique-qualities-Individual, Decide-Individual/Individual-Unique-Qualities, Unique qualities, Decide-Unique qualities/ Individual-Decide, Unique qualities-Decide, Decide/(I17/Physical, Spiritual, Healing)>Nutrition, Belief-integration-Nutrition, Spiritual-Nutrition/Nutrition-Belief integration, Belief integration, Spiritual-Belief integration/Nutrition-Spiritual, Belief integration-Spiritual, Spiritual/(I18/Totality, Wisdom, )>Mental-sense, Data-Mental-sense,/

TOUCH AND ENERGY

Quantum's: God and Self

>>>>Similar 2nd Elements>>>>(Family, God-head, Closed)>Mother, Son-Mother, Refuse-Mother/Mother-Son, Son, Refuse-Son/Mother-Refuse, Son-Refuse, Refuse/(Communicate, Meta Prog, Data Process)>Receive, Information patterns and storage-Receive, Storage models-Receive/Receive-Information patterns and storage, Information patterns and storage, Storage models-Information patterns and storage/ Receive-Storage models, Information patterns and storage-storage models, Storage models/ (Language, Message, Universal Language)>Energetic, Context-Energetic, Letters-Energetic/Energetic-Context, Context, Letters-Context/Energetic-Letters, Context-Letters. Letters/(Blocks, Data compression, Data comp. modes)>Minor, Distort-Minor, Programs-Minors/Minor-Distort, Distort, Programs-Distort/ Minor-Programs, Distort-Programs, Programs/(Human. Human Brain, Sensory Indicators)>Communication, Subconscious-Communication, Decision-Communication/Communication-Subconscious, Subconscious, Decision-Subconscious/Communication-Decision, Subconscious-Decision, Decision/(Memory, Change, Dimension)>Vicarious, Direction-Vicarious, Lateral-Vicarious/Vicarious-Direction, Direction, Lateral-Direction/Vicarious-Lateral, Direction-Lateral, Lateral/(Mind, Physical health, Spiritual health)>Emotion, Fitness-Emotion, Belief-Emotion/Emotion-Fitness, Emotion, Belief-Fitness/Emotion-Belief, Fitness-Belief, Belief/(Time, Nature, Reality)>Present, Patterns-Present, Time-Present/Present-Patterns, Patterns, Time-Patterns/Present-Time, Patterns-Time, Time/(Choice, Educate, Notes)>No Action, Sense of commonality-No Action, Senses-No Action/No Action-Sense of commonality, Sense of commonality, Senses-Sense of commonality/No Action-Senses, Sense of commonality-Senses, Senses/>>>>Unity second Elements>>>>(Disorder, Complete Disorder, Natural Man)>Skepticism, Randomness-Skepticism, Sympathies-Skepticism/Skepticism-Randomness, Randomness, Sympathies-Randomness/Skepticism-Sympathies, Randomness-Sympathies, Sympathies/(Entropy, Far from Equilibrium, Rock Bottom)>Norm, Chaos-Norm, Hopeless-Norm/Norm-Chaos, Chaos, Hopeless-Chaos/Norm-Hopeless, Chaos-Hopeless, Hopeless/(Self, Natural Man, Anomaly)>Myself, Doubt-Myself, Deviating-Myself/Myself-Doubt, Doubt, Deviating-Doubt/Myself-Deviating-Doubt-Deviating, Deviating/>>>>Integrate second Elements>>>>(Open System, Neg-entropy, Transformation Change)>Accept, Norm anomaly-Accept,

Heal Thy Self-Accept/Accept-Norm Anomaly, Norm Anomaly, Heal Thy Self-Norm Anomaly/Accept-Heal Thy Self, Norm Anomaly-Heal Thy Self, Heal Thy Self/(Space time continuum, Event, Expand)>Condition, Condition-Condition, Environment-Condition/Condition-Condition, Condition, Environment-Condition/Condition-Environment, Condition-Environment, Environment/ (Transformation, Correspondence, Transition Points)>Insert, Unity-Insert, Bifurcation Point-Insert/ Insert-Unity, Unity, Bifurcation Point-Unity/Insert-Bifurcation Point, Unity-Bifurcation Point, Bifurcation/(World-view, Age of Integrity, Integrate)>Family, Commonality Individual and Community-Family, Believe-Family/Family-Commonality Individual and Community, Commonality Individual and Community, Believe- Commonality, Individual and Community/ Family-Believe, Commonality of Individual and Community-Believe, Believe/(Physical, Spiritual, Healing)>Fitness, Belief Integration-Fitness, Energy-Fitness/ Fitness- Belief Integration, Belief Integration, Energy-Belief Integration/ Fitness-Energy, Belief Integration-Energy, Energy/

TASTE AND SMELL

Quantum's: Life and Death

>>>>Similar 3rd Elements>>>>(Family, God-head, Closed)>Child, Holy Ghost-Child, Repress-Child, Child-Holy Ghost, Holy Ghost, Repress-Holy Ghost, Child-Repress, Holy Ghost-Repress, Repress/(Communicate, Meta Prog, Data Process)>Message, Compressing for Model Making-Message, Transmission through language-Message/ Message-Compressing for Model Making, Compressing for Model Making, Transmission through language-Compressing for Model Making, Message-Transmission through language, Compressing for Model Making-Transmission through language/ (Language, Message, Universal Language)>Whole Body, Content-Whole Body, Numbers-Whole Body/Whole body-Content, Content, Numbers-Content/Whole body-Numbers, Content-Numbers, Numbers/(Blocks, Data compression, Data comp. modes)>Complex, Generalize-Complex, Models-Complex/Complex-Generalize, Generalize, Models-Generalize/ Complex-Models. Generalize-Models, Models/(Human. Human Brain, Sensory Indicators)>Body, Limbic-Body, Motivator-Body/Body-Limbic,

Limbic, Motivator-Limbic/Body-Motivator, Limbic-Motivator, Motivator/ (Memory, Change, Dimension)>Genetic, Role Model-Genetic, Depth-Genetic/ Genetic-Role Model, Role Model, Depth-Role-Model/Genetic-Depth, Role Model-Depth, Depth/ (Mind, Physical health, Spiritual health)>Body, Hygiene-Body, Closed Energy-Body/Body-Hygiene, Hygiene, Closed Energy-Hygiene/Body-Closed Energy, Hygiene-Closed Energy, Closed Energy/(Time, Nature, Reality)>Future, Processes-Future, Matter-Future/Future-Processes, Processes, Matter-Processes/Future-Matter, Processes-Matter, Matter/(Choice, Educate, Notes)>Let others take action, Belonging and harmonizing of a unique individuality with a sense of commonality-Let others take action, Pictures-Let others take action/Let others take action-Belonging and harmonizing of a unique individuality with a sense of commonality, Belonging and harmonizing of a unique individuality with a sense of commonality, Pictures- Belonging and harmonizing of a unique individuality with a sense of commonality/ Let others take action-Pictures, Belonging and harmonizing of a unique individuality with a sense of commonality-Pictures, Pictures/>>>>Unity third Elements>>>>(Disorder, Complete Disorder, Natural Man)>Mistrust, Deviating-Mistrust, Strengths-Mistrust/Mistrust-Deviating, Deviating, Strengths-Deviating/Mistrust-Strengths, Deviating-Strengths, Strengths/ (Entropy, Far from Equilibrium, Rock Bottom)>Success, Randomness Disorder-Success, Worthless-Success/Success-Randomness Disorder, Randomness Disorder, Worthless-Randomness Disorder/Success-Worthless, Randomness Disorder-Worthless, Worthless/(Self, Natural Man, Anomaly)>I, Limiting Beliefs-I, Plummet-I/I-Limiting Beliefs, Limiting Beliefs, Plummet-Limiting Beliefs/I-Plummet, Limiting Beliefs-Plummet, Plummet/>>>>Integrate third Elements>>>>(Open System, Negentropy, Transformation Change)>Express, Fulfill-Express, Know and Heal Others-Express/Express-Fulfill. Fulfill, Know and Heal Others-Fulfill/ Express-Know and Heal Others, Fulfill-Know and Heal Others, Know and Heal Others/(Space time continuum, Event, Expand)>Process, Outcome-Process, Self-Process/Process-Outcome, Outcome, Self-Outcome/ Process-Self, Outcome-Self, Self (Transformation, Correspondence, Transition Points)>Permeate, Integrate-Permeate, Crossover Points-Permeate/ Permeate-Integrate, Integrate, Crossover Points-Integrate/ Permeate-Crossover Points, Integrate- Crossover Points, Crossover Points/

(World-view, Age of Integrity, Integrate)>Society, Harmony of individual with community-Society, Choice-Society/Society-Harmony of individual with community, Harmony of individual with community, Choice-Harmony of individual with community/Society-Choice, Harmony of individual with community-Choice, Choice/(Physical, Spiritual, Healing)>Hygiene, Energy System-Hygiene, Physical-Hygiene/ Hygiene-Energy System, Energy System, Physical-Energy System/Hygiene-Physical, Energy System- Physical, Physical/ (Wisdom--)

➢ *(Arrow) indicates the next 3 Element sets in a continuum. The end of one set of 3 in a continuum and the beginning of the next in the continuum.*
*- (Hyphen) indicates the Elements continuum in their order. The – between the Elements also represents "Inter-relating, Interdependently". The Elements in the continuum do not change the meaning, identity, nor function of the other Element, they inter-relate, interdependently.*

, *(Comma)*

SOUND AND SIGHT

Algorithm/Continuum

First Elements Only:

>Father, Father-Father, Deny-Father/Father-Father, Father, Deny-Father/ Father-Deny, Father-Deny, Deny>Transmit, Data Processing-Transmit, Reception-Transmit/Transmit-Data Processing, Data Processing, Reception-Data Processing/ Transmit-Reception, Data Processing-Reception, Reception>Symbolic, Intent-Symbolic, Symbols-Symbolic/ Symbolic-Intent, Intent, Symbols-Intent/Symbolic-Symbols, Intent-Symbols, Symbols>Major, Delete-Major, Patterns-Major/ Major-Delete, Delete, Patterns-Delete, Major-Patterns, Delete-Patterns, Patterns>Identity, Mind-Identity, Reference-Identity/Identity-Mind, Mind, Reference-Mind/ Identity-Reference, Mind-Reference, Reference/(C6/Memory, Change, Dimension)>Real, Direction-Real, Height-Real>Mind, Nutrition-Mind, Body-Mind/Mind-Nutrition, Nutrition, Body-Nutrition/ Mind-Body, Nutrition-Body, Body>Past, Structure-Past, Space-Past/

Past-Structure, Structure, Space-Structure, Past-Space, Structure-Space, Space>Take action, Qualities-Take action, Music-Take action/ Take Action-Qualities, Qualities, Music-Qualities/Take action-Music, Qualities-Music, Music>>>>> Unity first Elements>>>>Doubt. Similar-Doubt, Uncertainty-Doubt/Doubt-Similar, Similar-Uncertainty-Similar/ Doubt-Uncertainty, Similar-Uncertainty, Uncertainty>Form, Stable-Form, Helpless-Form/Form-Stable, Stable, Helpless-Stable/Form-Helpless, Stable-Helpless, Helpless>Me, Frailty-Me, Similar-Me/Me-Frailty, Frailty, Similar-Frailty/Me-Similar, Frailty-Similar, Similar>>>>Integrate first Elements>>>>Admit, Form-Admit, Know Thy Self-Admit/Admit-Form, Form, Know Thy Self-Form/Admit-Know Thy Self, Form-Know Thy Self, Know Thy Self>Event, State-Event, Space-Event/Event-State, State, Space-State/Event-Space, State-Space, Space>Delete, Unity-Delete, Success-Delete/Delete-Unity, Unity, Success-Unity/Delete-Success, Unity-Success, Success>Individual, Unique-qualities-Individual, Decide-Individual/ Individual-Unique-Qualities, Unique qualities, Decide-Unique qualities/ Individual-Decide, Unique qualities-Decide, Decide>Nutrition, Belief-integration-Nutrition, Spiritual-Nutrition/Nutrition-Belief integration, Belief integration, Spiritual-Belief integration/Nutrition-Spiritual, Belief integration-Spiritual, Spiritual>Mental-sense, Data-Mental-sense,/

## TOUCH AND ENERGY

>>>Similar 2$^{nd}$ Elements>>>>Mother, Son-Mother, Refuse-Mother/Mother-Son, Son, Refuse-Son/Mother-Refuse, Son-Refuse, Refuse>Receive, Information patterns and storage-Receive, Storage models-Receive/ Receive-Information patterns and storage, Information patterns and storage, Storage models-Information patterns and storage/ Receive-Storage models, Information patterns and storage-storage models, Storage models>Energetic, Context-Energetic, Letters-Energetic/ Energetic-Context, Context, Letters-Context/Energetic-Letters, Context-Letters. Letters>Minor, Distort-Minor, Programs-Minors/Minor-Distort, Distort, Programs-Distort/Minor-Programs, Distort-Programs, Programs>Communication, Subconscious-Communication, Decision-Communication/Communication-Subconscious, Subconscious, Decision-Subconscious/Communication-Decision, Subconscious-Decision,

Decision>Vicarious, Direction-Vicarious, Lateral-Vicarious/Vicarious-Direction, Direction, Lateral-Direction/Vicarious-Lateral, Direction-Lateral, Lateral>Emotion, Fitness-Emotion, Belief-Emotion/Emotion-Fitness, Emotion, Belief-Fitness/Emotion-Belief, Fitness-Belief, Belief>Present, Patterns-Present, Time-Present/Present-Patterns, Patterns, Time-Patterns/Present-Time, Patterns-Time, Time>No Action, Sense of commonality-No Action, Senses-No Action/No Action-Sense of commonality, Sense of commonality, Senses-Sense of commonality/No Action-Senses, Sense of commonality-Senses, Senses>>>>Unity second Elements>>>>Skepticism, Randomness-Skepticism, Sympathies-Skepticism/Skepticism-Randomness, Randomness, Sympathies-Randomness/Skepticism-Sympathies, Randomness-Sympathies, Sympathies>Norm, Chaos-Norm, Hopeless-Norm/Norm-Chaos, Chaos, Hopeless-Chaos/Norm-Hopeless, Chaos-Hopeless, Hopeless>Myself, Doubt-Myself, Deviating-Myself/Myself-Doubt, Doubt, Deviating-Doubt/Myself-Deviating-Doubt-Deviating, Deviating>>>>Integrate second Elements>>>Accept, Norm anomaly-Accept, Heal Thy Self-Accept/Accept-Norm Anomaly, Norm Anomaly, Heal Thy Self-Norm Anomaly/Accept-Heal Thy Self, Norm Anomaly-Heal Thy Self, Heal Thy Self>Condition, Condition-Condition, Environment-Condition/Condition-Condition, Condition, Environment-Condition/Condition-Environment, Condition-Environment, Environment>Insert, Unity-Insert, Bifurcation Point-Insert/ Insert-Unity, Unity, Bifurcation Point-Unity/ Insert-Bifurcation Point, Unity-Bifurcation Point, Bifurcation>Family, Commonality Individual and Community-Family, Believe-Family/Family-Commonality Individual and Community, Commonality Individual and Community, Believe- Commonality, Individual and Community/ Family-Believe, Commonality of Individual and Community-Believe, Believe>Fitness, Belief Integration-Fitness, Energy-Fitness/ Fitness- Belief Integration, Belief Integration, Energy-Belief Integration/Fitness-Energy, Belief Integration-Energy, Energy/

TASTE and SMELL

>>>>Similar 3rd Elements>>>>Child, Holy Ghost-Child, Repress-Child/Child-Holy Ghost, Holy Ghost, Repress-Holy Ghost/Child-Repress,

Holy Ghost-Repress, Repress>Message, Compressing for Model Making-Message, Transmission through language-Message/ Message-Compressing for Model Making, Compressing for Model Making, Transmission through language-Compressing for Model Making>Whole Body, Content-Whole Body, Numbers-Whole Body/Whole body-Content, Content, Numbers-Content/Whole body-Numbers, Content-Numbers, Numbers>Complex, Generalize-Complex, Models-Complex/Complex-Generalize, Generalize, Models-Generalize/Complex-Models. Generalize-Models, Models>Body, Limbic-Body, Motivator-Body/Body-Limbic, Limbic, Motivator-Limbic/Body-Motivator, Limbic-Motivator, Motivator>Genetic, Role Model-Genetic, Depth-Genetic/ Genetic-Role Model, Role Model, Depth-Role-Model/Genetic-Depth, Role Model-Depth, Depth>Body, Hygiene-Body, Closed Energy-Body/Body-Hygiene, Hygiene, Closed Energy-Hygiene/Body-Closed Energy, Hygiene-Closed Energy, Closed Energy>Future, Processes-Future, Matter-Future/Future-Processes, Processes, Matter-Processes/Future-Matter, Processes-Matter, Matter>Let others take action, Belonging and harmonizing of a unique individuality with a sense of commonality-Let others take action, Pictures-Let others take action/Let others take action-Belonging and harmonizing of a unique individuality with a sense of commonality, Belonging and harmonizing of a unique individuality with a sense of commonality, Pictures- Belonging and harmonizing of a unique individuality with a sense of commonality/ Let others take action-Pictures, Belonging and harmonizing of a unique individuality with a sense of commonality-Pictures, Pictures>>>>Unity third Elements>>>>Mistrust, Deviating-Mistrust, Strengths-Mistrust/Mistrust-Deviating, Deviating, Strengths-Deviating/Mistrust-Strengths, Deviating-Strengths, Strengths>Success, Randomness Disorder-Success, Worthless-Success/Success-Randomness Disorder, Randomness Disorder, Worthless-Randomness Disorder/Success-Worthless, Randomness Disorder-Worthless, Worthless>I, Limiting Beliefs-I, Plummet-I/I-Limiting Beliefs, Limiting Beliefs, Plummet-Limiting Beliefs/I-Plummet, Limiting Beliefs-Plummet, Plummet>>>>Integrate third Elements>>>>Express, Fulfill-Express, Know and Heal Others-Express/Express-Fulfill, Fulfill, Know and Heal Others-Fulfill/Express-Know and Heal Others, Fulfill-Know and Heal Others, Know and Heal Others>Process, Outcome-Process, Self-Process/Process-Outcome, Outcome, Self-Outcome/

Process-Self, Outcome-Self, Self>Permeate, Integrate-Permeate, Crossover Points-Permeate/ Permeate-Integrate, Integrate, Crossover Points-Integrate/ Permeate-Crossover Points, Integrate- Crossover Points, Crossover Points>Society, Harmony of individual with community-Society, Choice-Society/Society-Harmony of individual with community, Harmony of individual with community, Choice-Harmony of individual with community/Society-Choice, Harmony of individual with community-Choice, Choice>Hygiene, Energy System-Hygiene, Physical-Hygiene/ Hygiene-Energy System, Energy System, Physical-Energy System/Hygiene-Physical, Energy System- Physical, Physical/ (Wisdom--)

# Chapter 21

## CHOICE

When Associated Quantum's are Bridgeable, we have less resistance in our lives. WE have less acts or instances of resisting or opposing forces in our lives. This refers to a mere psychological defense mechanism wherein one rejects, denies or otherwise opposes efforts to benefit them. Associated Quantum's as located on the Holographic Human Flat Map. Just having the Quantum's of Right and Wrong and then God and Self and then Life and Death able to bridge back and forth is the process of having these apparent opposites be able to go back and forth from one to the others.

Having Right and being able to discern, understand the Wrong possibilities and being able to have Wrongs returned to Right.

To join by providing a bridge, a passage through or over to the other. Being able to navigate, negotiate back and forth. The opposite of bridgeable is impassable. This bridging is created by a continuum of a coherent whole characterized as a collection, sequence, or progression of Values or Elements varying by minute degrees. Right and Wrong stand at opposite ends of a continuum instead of describing the two halves of a line (Wayne Schumaker). A compact set which cannot be separated into two sets neither of which contains a limit point of the other. The antonym of continuum is to cease.

The Law of Reverse Effect gives us Choice. The fact is that whatever program/model we have, we also have a complete opposite program already in the subconscious. The other programs must have permission from the conscious to be able to be accessed for conscious use. The opposite program/model is a result of the Reverse Effect Function the subconscious does with all data coming in prior to any of it being processed. The subconscious automatically does Reverse Effect. The Reverse Effect is Processing the information that came in, exactly as it came in, and completely opposite on every piece of information that came in. This is something the subconscious does automatically. Again, this is called Reverse Effect.

2 Nephi 2; 11: "For it must needs be, that there is an opposition in all things. If not so, my first-born in the wilderness, righteousness could not be brought to pass, neither wickedness, neither holiness, nor misery, neither good nor bad. Wherefore, all things must needs be a compound in one; wherefore if it should be one body it must needs remain as dead, having no life neither death, nor corruption nor incorruption, happiness nor misery, neither sense nor insensibility."

Reverse Effect is a helpful function done by the subconscious, there are great benefits to have the exact opposite of any data coming into the brain. Not only does this give us immediate choice, (depending on which data we have chosen to use) it creates an opposite program/model for every program/model you have. Change then really isn't that hard. What is hard is admitting and accepting that the program/model we use is the problem at all, in the first place. So quickly we blame the environment and others.

There are two things, we know of that stop the subconscious from doing this automatic process of Reverse Effect. One is "Absolute Truths", another is "Absolute Choice". There has to be a consistent pattern of absolute truths, or absolute choice, to get the subconscious to temporarily stop the automatic Reverse Effect long enough to get the next words into the subconscious and not be Reverse Effected by the subconscious process. Example:

There is a pattern of using absolute truths or absolute choice. It consists of a pattern of:

Five Absolute Truths

One Conscious Command

Four Absolute Truths

Two Conscious Commands

Three Absolute Truths

Three Conscious Commands

Two Absolute Truths

Four Conscious Commands

One Absolute Truth

Five Conscious Commands.

Absolute Truths might be a person's name, a direct quote of what they have said, the location, the environment, the date, what is, or just happened.

Conscious Commands generally are of a positive nature of what they may do, think, feel, or have.

Such as, "You are reading these words, words are letters put together in different sequences that have definitions, different letters each make a different sound when pronounced individually, there are allot of words made from the letters of the alphabet and you comprehend many words. Words are put together to create sentences when we write, words can be spoken, written or typed, text and your own ability to comprehend more and more words increases tremendously with greater conscious access. Different people put different words together in different ways, people might understand similar words in different ways and some words may sound like other words, and your abilities to comprehend, gain knowledge and wisdoms from language increases naturally within your own subconscious mind for conscious access. This is a written as an example of Truths with Conscious Commands you know these words and your ability to comprehended, open your mind, apply the information to gain knowledge and become wise increases naturally within you."

Throughout the scriptures the words of Christ are excellent patterns of this very structure. Absolute Choice examples are also in the words of Christ: "Could ye not." "If ye choose, ye may…" Using the absolute truth when speaking to others, using Absolute choice when speaking to others helps to open the conscious to greater subconscious data's.

Sometimes we may speak in Truths and Conscious Commands just naturally and your Wisdom increases as your knowledge grows from your application of the information from Data as simple as words, increasing you IQ and lifting you to limitless intelligence.

www.ingramcontent.com/pod-product-compliance
Lightning Source LLC
LaVergne TN
LVHW021705060526
838200LV00050B/2516